The Fire Ru

IAN M. FRASER

# The Fire Runs

*God's People Participating in Change*

SCM PRESS LTD

*To Allison, Sonaly,*
*Petya, Niall*
*and little Sheila –*
*shapers of the future*

334 00483 7
First published 1975
by SCM Press Ltd
56 Bloomsbury Street, London
© SCM Press Ltd 1975
Printed in Great Britain by
Northumberland Press Limited
Gateshead

# PENTECOST

Like fireworks lighting up the night
the Holy Spirit came:
dejected Christians felt the touch
of living fronds of flame –
and suddenly the world was young
and nothing looked the same

for Jesus' nearness gave them heart
to venture, come what would:
the love of Jesus bade them share
their house, possessions, food:
the mind of Jesus gave them speech
that all men understood.

This is the Spirit who, today,
new daring will inspire
and common folk are given gifts
to change the world entire:
the sparks which flew at Pentecost
started a forest fire.

I gladly acknowledge the use of material from WCC Study Encounters, especially nos. 39, 40 and 43; and songs for which Galliard hold copyright. In particular, I express my gratitude to Denise Whibley, secretary extraordinary and intelligent partner in the 'Participation in Change' programme; and to Julie Balley who helped to give the programme its first impetus.

# Contents

Testimony                                                            1

I  'I have come to set fire to the earth'                            3
   1  An End to Patronage                                            5
   2  An End to Theological Tribalism                               41
   3  An End to Missions and Mission Fields                         55

II  Our God, 'A Consuming Fire'                                     76
    4  The Place of the Poor                                        76
    5  The Claim of the World                                       87
    6  Principalities and Powers                                    91
    7  Sin, Wrath, Repentance                                       94
    8  Renewal                                                      99
    9  The Coming of Salvation                                     102
   10  The Blessing of Man                                         107
   11  The Character of Ministry                                   112

III  Hard Road Ahead: 'Be Salted with Fire'                       120
    12  The Role of Rejection in Response                          120
    13  The Role of Paralysis in Action                            124
    14  The Role of Non-communication in Prophecy                  128
    15  The Role of Conflict in Shalom                             133
    16  The Role of Powerlessness in Change                        139
    17  The Role of Conscientization and Dialogue in Mission and
        Evangelism                                                 143

Summons                                                            149

# Testimony

Can the same spring gush out fresh and brackish water? asks St James. From the same spring of experiences in Africa, Asia and Latin America I have returned refreshed and exhilarated, and full of grief and vomit.

My assignment, as co-ordinator of the 'Participation in Change' programme of the World Council of Churches, has been to contact people mostly at the bottom of the heap who, sparked and guided by some Christian motivation, seek to produce fruitful change in local situations – often under very severe pressures. This has brought me to fifty countries in four years, overwhelmingly 'Third World' countries; living, eating, sleeping wherever it might get me to the heart of some small movement or group of significance. To get in touch with a church like the one in Revelation, amazingly rich in its deeply impoverished life, and to see and hear and feel the damage done in the name of Christ through the centuries, has been for me a deeply formative experience.

There is this to say. There will be no health in the Western world until, in a new hearing of faith, the quality of life among the 'least of these' is understood, valued and appropriated and until we get off the backs of those we profess to be serving.

It has meant an awareness which can be conveyed much better by story than by analysis. It suggests fresh biblical dimensions. It issues in different perspectives on the struggle the church must engage in for a new world.

# I

## 'I have come to set fire to the earth'

A work camp took place on a Greek island. A building was constructed which could act as a school and serve for other communal purposes. From time to time, the work campers met with the village people. On one such occasion, through an interpreter, two young members from the USA described what life was like for them at home – detailing the many things that filled their day from dawn to dusk. At question time, a peasant woman rose. 'When do you live?' she asked.

In her book *Not Alone*,[1] Nan Partridge diagnoses in a group of despised Africans cycling to work, a despising of white superiors driving past in their cars: 'They look down on us, and not always with compassion, because we know so little how to live.'

There is undoubtedly a growing awareness in industrially advanced countries that affluence and sophistication do not of themselves bring people in any way nearer to the essential secret – how to live. What these parts of the world find hard to do is to look outside a charmed circle of approved people and accepted values and to seek what they lack in the lives of those who have been despised and disregarded.

Among the downtrodden there are styles of life which have a vitality and resilience which defy and overcome the impeding circumstances in which they have to be worked out. Why is it that, down the centuries, gipsies have been harassed and killed off, the church taking a leading part in the persecution? They are nonconformists. The societies around them are settled while they keep on the move. The people of those societies have a work routine, clocking on at a certain time of day, clocking off at another; while gipsies work in a long burst and then spend an equally long time enjoying the fruits of their labour in freedom from work. But note what is happening. Now it is a gipsy style which is being adopted by a more leisured society, with the use of caravans, the love of the open country, the refreshment of taking life as it comes instead of being ruled by the clock. How can we explain this contradiction? Is it that the basis of the ingrained resentment and hostility is the determination to treat as inferior an alternative way of life which insists on asserting disturbing but convincing values?

Often the underprivileged have gifts for living in community, making community and planning community, which advanced cultures have lost. To go through Port-au-Prince, Haiti, at night, is to find people spilled out from their poor homes on to the street, sharing jokes, telling stories, quietly or noisily linking up their lives with those of others. In many other countries where living conditions are cramped, the street affords space for making community, and people know how to use it creatively. In a *barrio* outside Santiago you find neighbours working with their sleeves up where anyone else needs a hand to build or mend his shack. Outside Lima, Peru, where the landless took over territory so that they might have somewhere to live, they themselves planned a satellite city, leaving space for broad avenues and areas of bare sand which are designated for communal meeting places and community activity.

The extended family is a way of living beyond your own body so that you have a great spread of roots from which to draw nourishment as well as a spread of branches which can provide shelter for many. This network of relationships is the strength of the poor. It may need to be re-received and re-created by societies which have dissected themselves into more strictly limited, functional relationships.

People often looked down upon because they lack formal education, are the artists and poets of the earth. Picasso was humbled by Australian aboriginal painting – it achieved so much that he had been searching after. An aboriginal map, utterly unlike a Western map, can show where food, water and game are to be found over a wide area, and still be an abstract painting to the eye. Music and dance provide the basic form of expression for many people in the Central American countries around the Caribbean. In Panama, a form of communal development of thinking and experience is provided by the building up of spontaneous poetic dialogue by two people who, in answering one another, discover a common theme; an intent crowd throngs around; and then when they reach a point of perception which everyone acknowledges, everything may end in a dance. In a Pentecostal community in Barquisimeto, Venezuela, a pastor was telling me about a conference they had held not long before. 'Would you like to hear the report?' he asked; then reached for his guitar and sang a song.

## 1  An End to Patronage

Authentic and free human beings stand on their own two feet before one another – and even before God – and look one another in the eye. What worse things can human beings do to others than to patronize them, or defer to them?

A patron is someone who imposes his desired form of relationship upon others. Inbuilt in patronage is the assumption of superior and inferior ways of life. The basis of the imposition is not analysis and assessment of alternative characteristics, belonging to different strata of society which build up or destroy the quality of life. It is a power basis. Those who hold power *place* others in a position of inferiority and dependency, and treat them accordingly. All goes well as long as the system is unquestioned by those who suffer under it. But, once they come alive and kick, hidden forces come into the open. The subtly oppressed undergo more naked oppression.

In the struggle through history between forces for righteousness and the down-drag of sin which is part of human make-up, man has gone through periods when it has been accepted that it belongs to the natural or even the divine order of things that there should be patrons and dependents. That time is past. Humanity has come to a new stage of awareness and growth.[2] A great deal of the turmoil of the world is due to this. Turmoil is no more unnatural or un-desirable than it is in a family when young people grow into adulthood and previous relationships have to be drastically revised.

It is part of the sickness of the church that it has so often acted through history as patron rather than as servant. It has used power-positions to make Christ's disciples into the church's dependents, twisting horribly the great commission in Matthew 28.18-20. All that is inherent in patronage has followed, including alliance with secular domesticating forces. When its position and security have been threatened, it has collaborated with these forces to safeguard its own situation. (But then, within its own life, there is an abundance of dependency and deference where there should be eye to eye meeting – imagine the disciples calling Peter 'Your Grace' or Paul saying he was going to Jerusalem to meet 'The Venerable, the General Assembly'.[3] The inner and the outer parts of the cup alike need to be cleansed.)

The church, which was called to be a lover of the poor, has so often acted as their patron. The poor are rising in revolt. It is a time when fresh opportunity is given to the church to turn again to servanthood. Will it grasp the chance? Concerned for its own place and security it has, in the past, been only too ready to bend its devices – authority, church machinery and theology – to justify a stance of continuing patronage. The test of a changed attitude will contain distinctive elements. Can the prestige churches of the West show a capacity to give new place to the poor; willingness to relearn from the lowly a sure touch for essentials; grace to regain wholeness in some of the world's dirty Jordans; readiness to be touched to new life by what the Spirit is doing in distant and neglected spheres? Are we, the brutal benefactors of history, now prepared to confess this sin – that we have set out to get, in so many lands, a dependent and easily manageable flock, and this – that we have been at least accessories (in the name of Christ!) in the disfigurement of humanity. Are we now prepared to throw our weight into ministries which release people's disturbing creativity, and pay the price of an increasingly critical relationship to powers-that-be?

## The Strange Place of the Poor

The existence of the poor in God's world and in his purpose is a riddle and a challenge.

Jesus said: 'Blessed are the poor' (Matt. 5.3; Luke 6.20). James wrote to the churches of his day the harsh words: 'You have despised the poor' (James 2.6). There is bite in these words. For Jesus and James speak, down the centuries, to contemporary humanity and the contemporary church.

The poor have their place in God's purpose – a special place. The neglected, the ignored, the discarded, the unimportant, the rejected, outcasts, drop-outs – according to the scriptures these are special people.

They are judges of the earth. They throw into vivid relief the righteousness and unrighteousness of men. Look at the way the poor are treated and you will know something about the judgment of God on the world, on us.

Their's is the kingdom. Only if we are lowly enough to receive from them will we be able to share the kingdom.

We who are differently situated[4] are not their patrons, but rather are in their debt: God's overwhelming love for the poor may be sufficient to rescue us as well.

There are parts of the riddle which are hard to bring together into one perspective. For a start, the poor seem to be treated as an economic class in the Bible, a quite definable grouping who have been trampled down and must be raised up. Yet in other ways, the word spills over. For it is a word of being set aside, whatever one's material condition.

The poverty of the economically poor is an unfreedom. But the

poor in the Bible are not only the materially poor. Others today
belong to the same category: peoples like the American Indians and
Australian Aboriginals whose cultures have been despised, or who
have been robbed of their own history by the imposition of alien
interpretations; those who have had indigenous forms of government and political life submerged by invading forms, as in parts of
Africa; those whose pattern of thought (e.g. in the Chinese part of
North Asia) or whose life-style (e.g. gipsies) has been discounted as
inferior. Within the ecumenical movement the poor are those
whose Christian worldview and manner of worship have been, like
that of the Orthodox, pushed on to the margins of what are considered the notable developments; Eastern Europeans who are made
to appear the poor neighbours of Western Europeans; those who are
disinherited because of language, or sex, or age. The poor are legion.
(Was it an awareness of these broader implications which led to
Matthew's text which reads the 'poor in Spirit'?)

Another part of the riddle is an imperative laid upon us at this
point of history to change drastically the relationship between the
poor and those who have displaced them from their position and
role in God's purpose. Thus:

The poor have a claim on the compassion and service of others.
But that is not enough.

The poor have a right to justice. True, but that is not enough.

The gifts of the poor need to be appreciated afresh. But that is
not enough, either.

The time has come for the poor to be given leadership in the
world community.

The rich world, in its poverty, needs to sit at the feet of the
poor world, with its riches, to relearn what human life is for.

There is a third part of the riddle. No romanticizing of the poor
will do. They may even have some kind of messianic role to fulfil
– they may be quite concretely the source of health, the bearer of
true values for the rest of society. Yet the poor are sinners like everyone else. Salvation is not of the poor. Salvation is of the Lord. Any
tendency to speak of the poor as if they were inevitably saved and
inevitable saviours may turn out to be part of a bourgeois action of
revulsion, a fairly painless guilt-compensation for the despising and
neglect which has been shown in the past. Its logic is to keep the
poor where they are and as they are. Why help a people to shed
poverty if it is in itself a means of grace?

To be treated as models and reminders to the affluent of alternative values and life-styles is a luxury which the poor cannot afford.
Their need is to escape. In any case, the strict logic would be that
all should become poor, not that one part of humanity be kept in a
certain state to be a reminder to others. Moreover millions of the

poor are so crushed, humiliated and ground down that it will take an intervention like that of Moses to enable them to lift their heads in hope.

The poor are human and sinful. Once their own lot improves, they, like others, often concentrate on improving it further, leaving their fellows in the dust. At a large farm taken over in Chile in Allende's time, the leader of the peasant commune emphasized that the struggle was still on. He named as enemies equally to be fought rich manipulators, bureaucrats and peasants-become-capitalists. No idealizing of the poor as such will do.

Then what makes the poor so important?

The gifts of the poor can prove a blessing to the whole human race. It is not that only the poor are gifted – all human beings are variously gifted. It is that, under the thought-control of dominating powers, the world has under-valued and set aside their gifts. In many cases these have been obliterated. In others they thrive tenaciously and can be a fresh resource for humanity, for true perspective and true joy in living. There is a call for reappraisal and fresh respect.

Already in Mary's vision of the world, God had put down the mighty from their seats and exalted those of low degree (Luke 1.46-53). The poor are a standing testimony to God's view of a world put right side up. It is for his human family to work with him to bring this about in all times and circumstances of history. The despising and disinheritance of the poor is a sign of disobedience, a pointer to the working of the wrath of God. Their honouring (not only in word – but by being *lifted* high) and reinheriting in human society is a sign of the breakthrough of the kingdom. There is a call to the church to amend its ways and put an end to a history of patronage towards the poor.

The great test may be for the poor to take leadership and for others to accept it. Possibly because the harsh struggle to live and be human presents alternatives starkly to them, they can show others the way to share bread, to make community, to tie words and acts into one bundle. They often possess that outstanding mark of leadership, the ability to sift out essentials from non-essentials, letting the latter drop into the background. But will they be able to retain these qualities when their situation improves? All of us must work sensitively together to cherish their gifts and respect their leadership so that that which has been won in poverty may not be lost in new status and greater acceptance. This applies equally within and between nations. It applies whatever category of people we speak about who are set aside and downvalued, the whole biblical range which embraces the word 'poor'.

The significance of the poor for the whole of humanity must be worked at in history. The riddle cannot be solved theoretically. Yet two things seem to be quite clear. The Spirit is pressing up to a re-evaluation of the downgraded; and is insisting that we get off their backs.

## A Sure Touch for Essentials

Among the lowly one finds a capacity to discern priorities with a simplicity which may look naïve, but which comes from concentrating on certain luminous and central things, paying attention to them as if they were jewels with many facets and fires, and letting other things fall into the background.

In a poor quarter in San José, Costa Rica, a woman of little education was sitting with a friend. Like all the houses around, her house was sub-standard and tiny for the eleven members of the family (plus myself) who lived there. Her husband had to be out at 5 a.m. each day and work till 7 p.m. selling vegetables, to support the family. They both belonged to a neighbourhood group trying to see what changes needed to be made in the area and how these could be brought about. The crucial part of the conversation started with the assertion that the community must be aroused to get a fairer deal. The friend protested that this was rather the responsibility of the local government officials. Then:

'Do you believe in Jesus Christ?'

'Yes.'

'Do you think Jesus Christ came to change life so that it was more the kind of life God wanted to see, or to leave it as it is?'

'I suppose to change it. Yes, to change it.'

'Do you think Jesus Christ meant to change life by himself, or did he mean us to share the work with him?'

(Hesitantly) 'I know he meant us to play a part.'

'Then how can you believe in Jesus Christ and let things stay as they are?'

The San Miguelito Community in Panama shares in the excitement of Roman Catholic lay people at having in their hands modern versions of the scriptures in their own language, Spanish. They still remember being told that they would go off their heads if they were to read the Bible directly. Everything had to be filtered through safe, priestly channels. Once the Bible was in their hands, they approached it as if it were a window from which to look out, see God, worship him and then discover what kind of life they should lead in consequence, starting from the very next step they had to take. They had no difficulties whatever about the early chapters of Genesis; they appreciated at once that questions were being posed to their own life through this story of the choices that human beings face generation after generation. One of the priests in the community, who also taught at a local seminary, was encouraged to gather a group of lay leadership and provide an introduction to these chapters. He spoke about their origin, composition, editing. When he ended there was a two-minute pause. Then people went straight to the question of what the chapters meant for worshipping God and for living out their lives in the world.

One of our major problems in the world is to know how to share bread. Nations are only beginning to learn, and have a very long way to go. It may seem easier to share bread with a neighbour in whom one can be in a face-to-face relationship. But those who, for months, have been living with the pangs of hunger will not agree. For sharing bread involves a serious disciplining of one's own desires and longings, a deep and compassionate awareness of the needs of others and a real willingness to put them first.

This quality seems to be much more often found among the poor. It is a gift constantly held out, if only the rich could learn to receive it.

Sitting on the floor of a Korean slum, a young man described his attempts to form a trade union outside the work premises after attempts to do this openly and publicly on the premises had been frustrated by intimidation and by 'promoting' leaders elsewhere. The move had been discovered, and he was dismissed from employment in a way which meant that no other firm was likely to take him on. That had been six months previously. There was no unemployment benefit.

'How do you manage to live?' he was asked.

'Fellow-Christians who do not have enough to eat themselves share what they have with me', he replied.

A group of about twenty-five people in Peru, several of them bakers, wanted to form a bakers' co-operative to provide bread at a reasonable price, also in the hope of being able to develop similar co-operatives elsewhere. But this seemed to be crying for the moon. As their own resources ran out, and their employment situation became desperate, it might have been thought that they would have grasped at any straw of hope, blown from any quarter. But they kept an amazing integrity while hope dwindled. When it was suggested to them that the World Council of Churches might provide the finance[5] to get their co-operative started, they reacted negatively. 'We have been manipulated for long enough and in all kinds of ways,' they said, 'no body like that, Christian or otherwise, ever gives money without wanting its own ends served. Everything has strings attached.' As their resources ran right out they kept alive a small flame of hope in their vision, with no idea how this could be realized but with an absolute refusal to sell their soul.

As long as some of them were employed, these shared with the whole group what they earned. But in time even these jobs were lost. Two of them, an ex-priest and a social worker, who had nothing more to live on, went to visit a friend of mine. He had had a birthday the previous day and offered two pieces of cake, knowing that they had probably had nothing to eat that day. They refused it. He pressed them, stressing that they would thus be joining him in his birthday celebration. The ex-priest replied, 'What would our stomachs feel like if we raised their expectations by giving them delicious food like that, and then made them face the want of tomorrow?'. So they refused the food. They also refused a loan of money. 'We must learn to live at the level of our impoverishment', they said.

'The church's laity here', said Francis Yip of Hong Kong 'are taken to be those who are pretty well off and can contribute substantially to the church, if they are inclined to do so. But the real laity are found among the workers, who would share their last crust with one another.'

At Guevara, La Paz, Tarlac, 230 kilometres out of Manila in the Philippines, a community of farm workers had suffered disaster after disaster. It started with a plague of rats, which, like locusts, ate right through their crops. Next year the rats came back and did the same thing. The following year, a virus destroyed the total crop. The year after that, typhoon and flood ruined everything. In May 1974 they were just beginning to get on their feet again. As catastrophe followed catastrophe, how did they react?

'Some of us were really, really afraid. For forty-five days, at the time of the typhoon, it rained day and night. I could not sleep for a whole month. I gathered my children and said "My children, maybe this is the end of the world".'

How did they survive through it all?

'We were able to save just a little of the harvest. A little help came from the government and other people. But when the floods came, we were very, very hungry.'

'I wonder if you believe me, but there were times during the flood I would cook one cup of rice for my nine children, including my husband ... one cup – and with the help of God, we did survive.'

Did they come to feel that God had laid a curse upon them?

'We felt God was punishing us for our sinfulness and carelessness', said one farm worker. His interpretation was at once challenged by others: 'God does not act like that ... God never acts like that. It wasn't a punishment, it was a time of testing. We had to go through a time of testing.'

And what had the time of testing done for them?

They had developed a new communal way of living. The few who owned their own fields decided to 'lend' their piece after the rice harvest to the farm labourers, who then planted mongo (beans). Some twenty-four hectares were put together and the neediest of the community got half a hectare to till. They now take common responsibility for the productive land. No one is ill or forced to go on a journey without neighbours stepping in and seeing that the land is tended. They are a community of caring and sharing and none is left out. Even the totally unemployed get their portion.

It was natural for them to have a service of worship when I arrived to consult with them. There was a hymn, followed by scripture reading. Then fourteen (out of a total company of forty) rose one after the other and built up an exposition of the scriptural text; and when the time for prayer came, as many took part. Living, worshipping, sharing possessions were all of a piece to them. There was not only a sure touch for essentials, but a vision of wholeness.

## A Vision of Wholeness

Things which we, in our traditions of the north, have split up, have been held together in maturer societies, like the one in La Paz.

'Why', said many Latin Americans, 'are you Europeans insisting that concerns of justice and the concern for the gospel should be interwoven, and wanting everyone to follow your new conviction? You can only put things together again if you have separated them. We never saw any reason for separating the gospel and justice from one another. To us they have always been two sides of one coin.'

The Orthodox churches emphasize the Christian vision of life as a vision of wholeness. Life has many parts but is one reality. To live life in Jesus Christ is to find a total integration of what had seemed separate.

One of the ways in which the Orthodox keep being marginalized in international conferences and gatherings is that the ground prepared for meeting, and the ambience of meetings, is not native to them. They have to fit in. They cannot be fully themselves.

Aware of this, the Association of Lay Academies and Centres for Social Concern went to Crete in 1972 for a world consultation – to shape out common plans and policies for the future. In the Gonia-Chania area, over the period of the Orthodox Easter, they were able to develop awareness of the particular flavour of one branch of Orthodoxy, and to find its expression of wholeness or 'togetherness'. The Monastery of Chania, dating back to 1618, houses monks who lead in worship and serve in the surrounding area as teachers, pastors and chaplains. In the diocese there are more than twenty free boarding schools with a total of about 2,000 scholars, many of them coming from remote farms and villages. An experimental farm serves also as an agricultural training centre; it aims to raise the level of animal stock in the diocese, to promote improved animal feeds, and to supply food for the boarding schools. To keep links with the mainland, and to get the vegetables to the mainland markets at their freshest, a 20,000 ton car ferryboat has been purchased – in which peasants and shopkeepers have invested their small savings, among the total of 3,500 shareholders. The first ever Orthodox Academy opens its doors to those who would know more about the Orthodox way of life, and to those who need to work out in dialogue diverse issues which confront them (a list of conferences includes the following: 'Christian Worship and Contemporary Man'; 'Woman in the Life of Society'; 'The Present and Future Situation of the Swine Industry on Crete'; 'Ministry in a Transformed World'; 'Problems of Greenhouses'; 'Artificial Insemination'; 'The Priestly Ministry Today'; 'The Priest's Wife in the Life of the Parish'; 'The Loom as a Source of Profit'; 'Technology and the Spiritual Life'). Not only is there an interwoven fabric of worship and work, education and prophecy – the very calendar they use, on this island which was under Turkish rule for 400 years, is a calendar of martyrdoms and must bring issues of the present into living relationship with the past. Crops and prayer, teaching and transport, past and present politics have a natural interrelationship.

A remarkable Evangelical Union of Pentecostal Churches in Venezuela, with its community centre in Barquisimeto, combines ecstatic worship, biblical preaching, schooling for deprived children and pressure against the exploitation of peasants in the country areas. Look at one of its conferences[6] and you will find the following features in some form or another: a base of biblical and theological reflection, an examination of features of community development and education; technical considerations – such as a better use of fertilizers – and worship. The first aim of the Community and Educational Centre, which works on a non-profit-making basis, is stated as follows:

To provide for the children of this area an integral education which harmonizes with the precepts of Christian education.

And the second: To help the campesino to liberate himself from the precarious situation in which he exists.

A group of unemployed youth, gathered at a centre to serve the needs of people like themselves in the city of Accra, Ghana, were asked what the next Assembly of the World Council of Churches should concern itself with. They answered: 'It should try to get Christians to understand the forces which make young people like ourselves waste their lives when they want to take their share of the work of the world. But there is one thing more important and

it must have priority.' 'What is that?' 'The World Council of
Churches must pray for us. We must all pray for one another in
the churches. We cannot do the other things the world needs
unless we pray.'

Towards the end of 1971 the first Aboriginal march of protest
in Brisbane took place. Its aim was a symbolic takeover of the
office of the government Adviser on Aboriginal Affairs, in order
to highlight his unwillingness to meet face to face with their
representatives, to draw attention to the fact that he and others
could over-rule even the most solemn decisions of the Aboriginals'
own Council, and to force the public into awareness of the wretched
treatment the original Australians received compared with whites.
Two hundred of them marched through the streets, breaking
windows and declaring to everyone that they had had enough.
The inevitable confrontation with the forces of law and order came
as they drew near their goal. In the scuffles which broke out nine
were arrested.

To initiate this manifestation of their growing anger, they had
met in church for a service of worship and a last-minute check-up
on strategy and tactics.

'But why should you go to church first of all?' asked a surprised
enquirer.

He was met by surprise in his turn. 'What is there to do in a
situation like ours', an Aboriginal replied, 'except to commit your
cause to God and then go out and get your heads broken by the
police?'

A cluster of four villages in Bungsipsee in Chaiyapoom Province
in North-East Thailand – an area of protected forests where tigers,
bears and elephants still roam at large – invited a student team to
live with them and work with them in the development of their
common life. The enterprise attracted students from all the universi-
ties of Thailand. It was sponsored by Roman Catholics; but
Buddhists in the team outnumbered Christians by five to one. The
students worked in the fields with the youth of the villages, twelve
of whom lived in the camp each week and represented a potential
force for understanding and initiative once the students had gone.
The villagers worked with the students on the construction of water
tanks to anticipate and provide for periods of drought. They
consulted together. They shared their different skills. Tiny girls
who had never handled a mattock in their lives, soon learned the
swing which puts the work on the iron head rather than on human
arms; and grew adept at working in cement and concrete.

It was part of the new and hopeful movement of students
towards industrial and rural workers, in identification and concern.

It was an exercise in mutual respect and understanding between people of different faiths. In the morning the flag was raised and people gathered round for a short period of Buddhist prayer and meditation. Each evening, after an evaluation session, Christians were accustomed to hold an act of worship. But after some time Buddhist students said 'Many of us believe in God too; may we join in?' They were welcomed. Soon Buddhists were reading Old and New Testament lessons, singing hymns, offering prayers as part of a total trusting company. The villagers clearly felt themselves under no proselytizing pressure. One of the last acts was the cleaning and clearing of the grounds of the village temple at the request of the Buddhist priest. People shared more and grew in understanding more by working together than they ever could by simply talking together.

It was an exercise in human development. The villagers had their lives enlarged. But the students probably gained more than they gave. 'For many of them', said Father Laschenski, the priest who helps to spark the enterprise and who takes his share in all the work, 'this is a first contact with rural people, especially poorer people. They get their eyes opened. They begin to think of the whole Thai community. They also learn to respect the wisdom and values of villagers. They go back much more fully developed human beings.'

It was a politicizing exercise. When headmen and village representatives met the others in council, they would identify their needs – more land or more productivity from the existing land; water for irrigation, probably a small dam; health care – in their area there was not one doctor for 70,000 people; appropriate education. They would then ask their new friends if they could do something with the authorities to actualize these hopes – authorities of whom they themselves lived in fear. Gently the ball would be passed back to their feet and encouragement given to analyse their situation, sort out priorities, determine concrete action and deal with authorities – as people who had a thought-out case to state. The result was that the villagers before the end of the enterprise came out of their separateness and formed a working team to look at the total needs of the four communities; and were finding courage to approach the forestry commission for land and other authorities for agricultural and sanitary advice and aid, offering to contribute physical work and materials themselves.

It was an exercise in wholeness. Village sanitation and personal health care, manual work in common, awareness of needs and humble listening on the part of those thought to be more expert, growth in confidence towards common consultation and action, worship and prayer, Christian/Buddhist understanding, theological reflection (stimulated by the hostility of some opponents of the project), song and dance (both Thai and Western), personal and social development – were all woven in one fabric. Here was a drawing together of things which are often broken apart, a loving, imaginative outreach on the part of a small band of Christians who really cared for the wholeness of the human community.

If you would find maturity in Christian living, living which is all of a piece, in which faith and its expressions are in unity, you can find it in the world church. But you must be humble enough to go, not where you want to find it, but where it is to be found. It is the meek who shall inherit the earth. How much longer are we in our part of the world going to ask those who have written convincing papers on our loss of quality and wholeness of life, self-confessed bankrupts, to write fresh papers on how to recover these? We must seek not fresh papers but fresh sources. How long are the churches of the West, so clearly anaemic because of their loss of a touch for essentials and their loss of a vision of wholeness, going to deprive themselves of the blood which members of the same world family, poor but rich in red corpuscles, can give them?

## Parables of New Life

### 1. San Miguelito

In the elemental struggles in which many Christians are engaged today, new styles of life are being worked out and solutions found by the simple which still elude the wise and prudent. As people struggle, they bind together faith and politics; rediscover the foreign missionary as a short-term expendable leader; redesign the ordained ministry to be a humble, enabling form of service; experiment with many types of lay ministry – sometimes driven to brilliance by the obstacles put in their way by the institutional leadership; and tackle the biblical and theological understanding of their faith. They make of life itself a single, total liturgy as they draw the riches of their culture into acts of worship and emerge, reinforced, to live a more authentic life as the people of the land – with a particular history to deal with and yet members of a universal Christian family.

### Interview with a member of the San Miguelito Community (1972)

Q. How did the parish of San Miguelito start?
A. It began with an invasion of people from the interior and from certain areas of Panama City, who were forced by the wretched conditions of life to look for room – space to live. They moved into

this pastureland area where there were already a few scattered homes.

They showed a real sense of adventure, a spirit and faith in what they could become somewhere else. It was an exodus for them, an exodus from the interior where they were tied to land which would never be theirs, or an exodus from the city where they would live with perhaps twelve people in a room, the kids sleeping on shelves in the wall, no plumbing, no conveniences, so close that there was no way of living humanly. They came here because they began to see that there *was* a way to have some space.

Legally, they were outlaws, because they were squatting on land that wasn't theirs. But the government established the *Instituto de Vivienda y Urbanización*, which began to buy the land and allocate it to the people. (They pay back regularly a certain amount of money to clear off the loan.) It came out very well for some. But there is still a lot of land that people really cannot say is their own, and the basic planning questions haven't yet been resolved.

Q. What about the church: how did it move in?
A. It was a co-operative effort between the diocese of Chicago and the diocese of Panama. Three priests from Chicago were invited to come by the Bishop of the City of Panama. They arrived not really knowing exactly what to do for the best. So they had to go round asking people.

The very basis of culture in Panama is dialogue, conversation, dance, music. Everything comes from what two or three or four or five people do together, what they create together. Thus the three priests, seemingly by accident, hit upon the key to the whole approach. They had to begin with the people, and create.

The people began to talk about their faith, and what they could become through these changes. Out of this grew a series of prepared discussions. As it turned out, the more planned gatherings provided the basis for advance in any sector of the life of San Miguelito you care to name.

The consciousness of the people began to grow. The basic desire in the work of the church at that moment of time, I think, was to help people to comprehend the faith that made them move. What led them to make a change so radical in their lives – to leave land on which they and their fathers had lived and had suffered tremendous oppression? What were they really looking for? Faced by these questions people came to the realization that they were looking for something *great* – not just for something good, but for something *great*. This willingness for radical change laid the basis for the church in San Miguelito at that time.

From all this came a movement of the people to *be* the church,

to *feel* the church, to *preach* the church and the risen Lord. They
began to handle these courses themselves. They began to be the
real carriers of the message of salvation (in the complete sense,
salvation of the whole man). Out of this evangelical movement
there then emerged a strong political movement.

There really wasn't much faith in what the government was
doing, or in the possibilities for the future. But, once awakened,
people began to talk about the Constitution and what it meant;
the Canal Zone Treaty, what the presence of the Americans in
the Zone meant; what the situation of oppression was in the country
areas and in the city. The whole situation of the country began
to be discussed in weekend sessions. From this emerged an intense
conviction that they themselves had to take decisions regarding
their own political life, as well as about church life. They were
priests, prophets and political leaders because they were the people
of God.

When the overthrow of Arnulfo Arias took place in 1968 and
the Panamanian colonels took over the government, there was a
strong protest from the San Miguelito people. About 5,000 of
them took part – young people as well as old men and old women –
in a march which was stopped by the guardia. They threatened to
blow the people off the street. They didn't do it, and eventually,
after consulting with the central headquarters, they let the march
go on. But it was a big problem for the government. The next
day they called the men down and threatened them, trying to scare
them; but they all stood firm and said, 'If there is any change in
government the people should have a say in it. And if you are
going to have a revolution, well, revolution without popular participation is nothing, so forget it.' Nobody backed down. As a
result, the government began a series of conversations with the
people. What came out of that was an agreement that they should
have their own Assembly.

The elections went off well. About 76% of the people who were
able to vote, voted; and the Assembly was constituted. But from
that moment up to now (November 1972) there have been a series
of betrayals by the national government. All the promises were
broken. Yet the 'conscious' people (some others gave in to their
fears) decided: 'If we can't do anything right now, while we are
oppressed by force, let's develop our own awareness of life, our
ability to celebrate life, our understanding of what we are suffering
– and prepare our people for another step in faith, so that when
the Lord comes in some particular action, some particular event,
we will be ready.' This outlook is basic among the men who work
as volunteers in the different parishes. They are not only preparing
for the diaconate but also preparing for some new God-given

opportunity in history, which they are sure is going to come.

Q. You mention a diaconate. Do you have deacons?

A. A sizable number of people were trained as deacons. The bishop took the reports and petitions to Rome – which were very formal, very definite. He lost them all somewhere between here and Rome. Anyway, they never arrived where they were supposed to go. There were six or seven copies and he lost them all. After waiting and waiting, the men finally said, 'Let's cut this out. Let's have a lay ministry. Forget about the diaconate.' So we set them apart and they just got on with the job. About 250 trained volunteers are now carrying substantial responsibilities, supported by the core group of full-time priests and laymen.

Q. How are these ministries developed so that they relate to actual needs?

A. We find people taking on themselves a ministry based on what has been their own personal experience of resurrection in a particular area of their life. For instance, Fidel Gonzales is extremely adept at talking to people who are sick and dying, who need someone to put an element of hope in their lives. Fidel is good at this because he himself has twice been close to death. A car turned over and he was almost killed. His brain was badly damaged; one side was knocked out and the doctors thought he wouldn't be able to speak. However he is left-handed, and as there is some kind of relationship between the right side of the brain and the left side of the body, he came out of it. It was an experience of resurrection for him. Slowly he learned to walk again, to write again. To hear him talk about his own experience, or talk to a person about what sickness implies, what death and the resurrection mean, is a fantastic experience because *it is something that he has lived*. He can fulfil ministry in this particular way.

Favio and Adelina are a couple who have lived out the difficulties of marriage. This is a second marriage for Adelina. The first was an absolute disaster. To find in a marriage relationship what she has found with Favio! Then to see what Favio has become! Here is a man who stutters badly, and all of a sudden there he is, standing up and performing a liturgy of the word, giving communion to an area group! This all comes out of the reality of resurrection in marriage, resurrection in a portion of life which they have lived out together.

Hear Favio talks to a young couple who are going to be married – this man who really couldn't speak before: 'Now look, marriage is a completely different experience, nobody can tell you what it is going to be like. It is going to be yours. You must put the

### A house church at worship

One night when a planned engagement fell through, I wandered among the homes of the community. There I met a man I had previously talked to as he was washing down a car. Nine months ago he had been a hopeless drunk. Now he lived by doing odd jobs. I asked if there was anything happening which I could attend. He said he was a lay minister and was just going to conduct a liturgy of the Word. I would be welcome to come along. He was still in the same creased shirt and trousers in which he had washed the car.

The bare house in which we met was really one small room, with two partitions breaking it up – one for a bedroom, the other probably for a bedroom or kitchen. For a good part of the service, two of the children of the household were crying intermittently: occasionally one would get up to pull back the curtain and gaze at us. Outside dogs barked and howled, competing with a transistor radio. On the kitchen table was a cross, with a lighted candle on either side. Over his opennecked shirt, Bill placed a 'yoke' or stole and was ready to start. About ten neighbours pressed in, some bringing their own chairs or stools with them. I shared with an older man a couch whose middle had the flock showing through. Most of those who took part were in their twenties or early thirties.

There was an introductory section in which people sang and gave responses. Then a passage from the Acts of the Apostles, used throughout the parish that week, was taken for study. Practically everyone participated in building up an understanding of the passage. At one point Bill seemed to be pushing them too strongly in emphasizing God's presence in the midst of life. They would not have it. 'We know God is in the thick of things where we are', they said, 'We believe that. But that is not all. God is also beyond us. We don't know *how* he can be with us and beyond us. But that's just the way it is.' After about forty minutes of Bible study, those who took part were asked to offer prayers and all but two responded. Another song was sung, there were one or two more responses, and the service ended.

elements of creativity in it.' To listen to him speak to those about to be married is something to live for!

You find in the group people who have a clear vision of where we should be going. Chado is recognized not only in San Miguelito but by the laymen in all Panama as the person they most want to listen to, and to tell their troubles to, and to have him say where we are all going. He has a tendency to shy away from this, he is afraid of this kind of power. But if there is a man with the ability and the vision of bishop in Panama, he is the one.

One of the things that is so fascinating about San Miguelito is the fact that people have a deep understanding of scripture. For instance, Modesta Contreras is a man who didn't know how to read. His fascination with scripture led him to make the decision to learn, but he reversed the usual man-woman role and learned from his wife. This changed his whole life. Now, his love of scripture and his ability to express himself are something fantastic.

Q. Do the people see a theological dimension in their discoveries?

A. I think that there are some definite points at which people are beginning to see some theological depth in what they are living. The element of physical change had been a basic thing for them. They went on from that to the realization that profound, permanent, definite, personal change is deeply important in life. They applied this perception to the context of their family, and families began to change. They put it in the context of the community, and realized that together they must become agents of change. They discovered that there were changes which God intended to bring about – that this is how he relates himself to the world – and knew that they were called to share in his work to change all life.

Another question which preoccupies people is 'What are we really living for?' They recognize that there are a lot of people who just live to survive and a lot of people who live just to get on – but that an extremely important element of life is to live for other people. If we are to be Christians we have to strive for that. The idea of living with an intense personal concern for other people, with an intense personal preoccupation for union with other people, is a crucial insight.

Two more points that we could easily identify as theological understandings are people's *preoccupation with the incarnation* – as a reality which does not just belong to Jesus the Lord, but is still shared with mankind – and the *presence of a creative spirit* in a community, when it is conscious of its faith and of its responsibility as something able to change the world. There is no preoccupation with a God who is outside the world. They believe in a God who is very definitely incarnate in present reality and who represents the possibility of change. There is consciousness of the fact that the Lord is going to do the changing, and that they are working with him. There is an intense respect for the change that is to come, whatever it will be. But at the same time there is complete conviction that God is somehow present in the world, and that for this reason they should have faith.

Q. Do people build up the worship of the parish themselves?
A. The basic lithargy we have is the lithargy in the different sections of the parish, which the people prepare themselves in small groups. It is here that the relationship of concern is established, together with a desire to praise. They deepen their understanding that when a prayer is made it is made to the Lord who is present, and the community must begin to look for ways to live it out. But the basic structure is rather classical.

The main liturgical contribution of the people came about very, very slowly – it was something indigenous. Some of the men in the community who played the guitar and drum, or the local folk instrument, the *bocina*, felt that the music they were singing in liturgical services wasn't really theirs. Their music was basically very simple dance music, but music which called for creation and participation. So they began to choose folk melodies that came from their grandfathers and their greatgrandfathers, and to pick out different sounds that would express basic ideas – penitence for instance.

In the *Misa Tipica*, in 'Lord have mercy', there is a kind of yodel called the *Saloma*, which plaintively expresses the deep cry of need, of pain – the need for change and pain that things don't change. The response to this cry is 'Glory to the Lord!'. The understanding of the people is that the cry of pain brings an immediate answer from the Lord who lives in pain, who is here in the midst of change. When one realizes that the Lord is present with you in it all, you have immediate reason to rejoice.

Q. Do people dance in any of the liturgies?
A. Yes, on special occasions, at the offering of the gifts. What happens is that there is a moment in the liturgy where the people say, 'We want to give something; what is the thing that is most ours?' Well, it's dance. So a couple or a group will dance as a presentation, to make an offering. This happens for instance at the Feast of the Resurrection of the Lord. At Christmas, it is done in a sort of pageant. The people work out different reactions to the reality of the incarnation according to their own rural folk tradition. After the reading of the gospel there is a presentation of

gifts to the Lord who is one with them again. It takes the form of a dance.

We had a marriage here at Pentecost. Pentecost is a great feast; it is actually the *fiesta* of the patron of our church. We didn't want to march around with statues of saints – it is hard to have the Holy Spirit incarnate in a piece of wax! But we had a wedding – a young couple who could dance very well. They decided to get married in rural costume, their real dress. They danced the offertory. It was beautiful, because it really expressed what they felt towards each other; and in their faces, in their way of dancing, you could see the desire to create together. The coming of the Spirit became vivid through their own relationship, their relationship to the people, their offering of both to God.

## 2. *The Tondo People*

In Manila, the Philippines, a squatter community of 60,000 people is getting a name for itself. Zone I Tondo is a narrow strip of land reclaimed by the government as part of a plan to expand and improve the port facilities. The people have created an effective organization called, for short, ZOTO.[7] The Tondo people have been trying for twenty years to get legal title to their land and have resisted all efforts to dislodge them. An earlier organization had succeeded in mobilizing more than 5,000 grass roots people for a rally which focussed on the land problem on 16 March, 1970 at the Malacanang Palace. Although this enterprise disintegrated through inexperience and a certain measure of corruption, the more powerful ZOTO came into being just in time – in October of the same year. Shortly after it was constituted, the worst typhoon in fifty years hit the area, and 2,000 homes were smashed. So effectively did the organization cover the community that it took only one day to estimate accurately food, clothing and shelter needs and contact relief agencies – so that 5,000 sheets of corrugated iron, for instance, were obtained and fairly distributed.

Ten days later the Pope visited Manila. The people got wind of it that Tondo was on his visiting agenda. To the horror of the local hierarchy, ZOTO declared themselves the appropriate body to welcome the Pope; and declared their intention of asking his blessing on their struggle for land rights. In the end, Mrs Herrera, the President, did accord the welcome, and he did bless their struggle to get title to the land on which their shacks were built.

From the beginning an ecumenical team of Roman Catholics and Protestants, the Philippine Ecumenical Council on Community Organization (PECCO) was brought into being to provide a community organization staff training facility, so that the people

might be helped to identify the problems and be able to get advice
on possible lines of action. The understanding on which PECCO
worked was that the people themselves were the best judges of
their own needs, and that the people themselves, operating as an
organized, cohesive force, offered the best means of achieving
fulfilment of those needs.

Since then, ZOTO has tested its strength. Early in 1971, a bill
placed before the Congress, aimed at creating the Tondo Development Authority, which would have turned Tondo land into a
business empire and a tourist spot, was defeated, largely by a
people's lobby. In June 1972 ZOTO staged a three-day picket
against the Cement Association of the Philippines Corporation
(CAPC) which had obtained a lease of land without going through
the recognized processes and consulting the people who would
have been affected; 3,000 people then joined in a peaceful
demonstration. A meeting with the Corporation proved to be fruit-
less, and ZOTO representatives felt they were simply being fobbed
off. So, since the lease of land was closely related to port development, and this hinged on a loan from the West German government, the German Embassy was approached, and a meeting
arranged with the Reconstruction Loan Corporation, the financing
company. At a meeting on 6 November, 1972, a halt was called,
and an assurance given that ZOTO would be fully consulted before
the implementation of any government project affecting them.

Now there are nearly one hundred local groupings each covering
one compassable part of the total geographical area; and an assembly
meets once a year to shape out policies which are in accord with
the minds of representatives of these organizations.

Here was a situation in which people who were without rights,
were afflicted by poverty, unemployment, malnutrition, seemed
to be an inevitable prey to apathy. How could they, terrified in the
beginning even to encounter officialdom, come to the point where,
to signal all end to servility, they replaced the phrase 'we request'
by the phrase 'we demand'?

There was a stubborn remnant of those who, over years of hopes
and dashed hopes, refused to be cowed; and were alive to the
opportunities presented by such events as the Pope's visit.

There was a supporting church team, of social workers and other
resource people.

The people were helped to tackle small gains before reaching for
greater gains. Thus they would see the need for piped water or
electricity, which reached a certain point, to be extended to cover,
say, twelve more houses. In great trepidation, they would face
a man behind a desk with a carpet on the floor, breaking into a
world which to them was unfamiliar, in which they were ill at ease.

Taking their courage in their hands, they would state their case – and discover, as if it were a new thing, that they had a good case, discover that the law might be on their side, discover they could stop destructive action or get changes made. So they grew in confidence and tackled bigger issues.

They had a special way with those who might have been thought of as their benefactors.

After the typhoon, in order to be in a position to deal with any future disasters, ZOTO asked relief agencies to channel their provision through ZOTO. Church World Service refused the demand, and the delegation who approached the director felt they had been brusquely treated. So a picket was organized in front of the headquarters of the National Council of Churches, where Church World Service had its offices. The protest was effective.

Cardinal Santos, then Cardinal-Archbishop of Manila, who had earlier paid little attention to the people's plea for help in getting land rights, was placed in an embarrassing position by the Pope's sympathetic reaction to the people's needs. Not long afterwards he unilaterally announced a large-scale housing project for the area. ZOTO denounced this as 'another traditionally charity-oriented programme, ignoring the expressed wishes of the people and their right to participate in the planning of their own future'. They would have none of it. Instead, they went to the 'open house' which the Cardinal traditionally held on Christmas Day, carrying bags of earth (if the Cardinal was to go ahead with his housing scheme, he would need Tondo soil on which to build it!) and demanding, among other things, that he support the establishment of a ZOTO non-profitmaking housing corporation.

In spite of promises that it would respect the land on which the people lived, and take note of the potential need for the use of any vacant land which might be available for people displaced by port development and roads, – in March 1971, the government began to build a warehouse on a vacant piece of ground known as Parola Compound. ZOTO swung into action immediately. It divided up the land in question and allotted space to an appropriate number of families, who were invited to go and construct houses or shacks, thus pinning out the disputed site. The people moved in, and had just constructed frameworks when the police appeared. They stopped, frightened. Believing that iron needed to be put in the people's wills, the ecumenical support team threw down a challenge. The construction had to proceed by a certain deadline, or they would withdraw their support from this particular enterprise. There was hot debate, but the deadline came and went without further action. The wisdom of the team was confirmed when the government moved in and easily cleared the ground of the flimsy frameworks.

But then a delegation went to meet with the team. They said something like this: 'You may have been right in the advice you gave us. But you put pressure on us to meet the deadline *you* chose. We want you to understand that it is not your future, it is not your homes which are at stake, it is ours. We would rather make bad decisions which we have come to in our own way and in our own time than good decisions which have been made for us. We are not prepared to have you think for us and act for us and put pressure on us. We will take responsibility for our own future.'

### The Brutal Benefactor

*A man's standing before God is related to his standing among men.* Those who think they are worth nothing and have nothing to contribute, who are made into mere receivers, need to rehear the song of reversal 'the humble have been lifted high' (Luke 1.52); 'You are therefore no longer a slave but a son' (Gal. 4.7); 'Here is the message of the First and the Last, who was dead and has come to life again; I know the trials you have had, and how poor you are – *though you are rich* ... (Rev. 2.8-11).

In a contribution to a consultation of Missionary Societies in Selly Oak Colleges, Birmingham, in March 1974, Professor Miguez Bonino, from the Argentine, was asked to suggest any way in which development aid might be given and received so that a healthy relationship was seen to exist between the giver and receiver. He said: '... when it creates a rightful sense of defiance, a sense of lack of respect ... when aid helps people to become a self-asserting community which takes initiatives, there is a liberating context in which a liberating gospel may be preached.'

But the church, that brutal benefactor, has shown its preference for a docile people. They are more easily managed. The poor have come to believe, and use the words as if they had thought of them themselves and had applied them to themselves, instead of being cajoled into them: 'We are just the humble of the earth. Our part is to obey and follow. Life will be hard here. But God will make up for it beyond death.' They have been taught to be fatalistic, submissive. Their human birthright has been taken from them, in the name of Jesus Christ!

Those who protest and stand against the tide can be relocated or otherwise silenced.

When Father Wuytack from Belgium lived among the poor in Caracas, Venezuela, this provided such a challenge to the traditionalist church that he was removed. The poor joined ranks with students and priests to protest against his removal and demand un-availingly, his return. About a year later, of nineteen priests who had signed a petition that he be permitted to continue his work, all but one had been allotted responsibilities elsewhere.

Another sign is the ambivalent attitude to laity. There is evidence of a genuinely fresh appreciation of the total resources of the church, and the need to bring them into play. But with this goes a desperate worry about a membership which may no longer be kept at heel. Laity Councils and Commissions sometimes offer a way of escape – means to tidy lay people safely into the system. Another way is offered where church authorities organize and train lay men and women – happily, this may keep one end of the rope in the same hands as before, even though it is a longer rope.

But the starkest example of the church's choice of the role of patron rather than servant, has been in the field of politics. Through the centuries, the church has taken sides. Through the centuries it has denied that it takes sides. It is adept at self-deception. It has no alternative but to take sides.

Consider 'Scottish oil'. The development of oilfields brings with it considerations of employment, growth of local industries, drastic change in many local communities, preservation of the environment, short-term and long-term gains, a new power-base to adjust power imbalance in the United Kingdom – many matters which affect the wellbeing of Britain and of Scotland in particular. Multi-national companies involved in extraction need to be given a fair crack of the whip and, at the same time, must have their ruthless profit-making drive tempered to the needs of the human community. A church can take sides in three possible ways. It can support the multinationals (maybe getting in return a chaplaincy service to oilmen). It can be neutral. It can get involved, digging into the issues and lending its weight to this side and that to help justice to be done.[8] The first two ways – co-operating and staying neutral – are ways of giving multinational companies unqualified support. Consider the case of a company which wants to build a terminal on a scenic strip of coastline, against the wishes of the local people. Such is the finance and power this vast organization can muster that to give full support or to stay out are equally means of giving it its head. Neutrality is a way of giving in to power and money pressures, of making straight the way of the powerful.

One of the marks of the church (which would not have been recognized by the early apostles!) has been direct collaboration with the powers-that-be, or the adoption of a position of neutrality which has given them their will. The result has been what sick-at-heart Christians in many lands have described as the complicity of the church in the repression and disfigurement of humanity.

The church cannot stay out of politics. If it claimed, in Jesus Christ, a hole-in-the-corner spiritual leader who extended his title only to individual and family life, it might attempt this. But if it sees in Jesus Christ the one who can bring the whole world to fulfilment, it has to accept the scope of the Old Testament, of Romans, Colossians and Ephesians, as the sphere of his operations – and be prepared for whatever scale of involvement he requires of it. When, in 1971, the Roman Catholic Council of Bishops in Chile came out in favour of a non-political priesthood, this meant in effect that priests should not be *left-wing*. No more than that. Words, deeds and silences of the church and its ordained servants have political weight, inevitably.

If the Roman Catholic Church illustrates this particularly, it is only because of its size and its centralization of power, which inevitably makes it a force which secular authorities will want to have on their side, or to neutralize. But the establishment status of the national churches in Scotland and England, and the financial tie-up with the state of many continental churches, bring similar threats to their independence and integrity.

Attention has been focussed recently on the secret Vatican-Portuguese Accord of 1940. It represents a close tie-up between church and state. Article II of the Accord says: 'Portuguese Catholic missions are considered to be of imperial usefulness; they have an eminently civilizing influence.' Article VI says: 'Foreign missionaries will be subject to local prelates and must make a statement of renunciation of the laws and tribunals of their own countries, and submit themselves to Portuguese laws, by which they will be judged.' Article XIX states: 'Bishops and governors will all have the same salary, except in a colonial capital. The salaries of ecclesiastics will be the same as for state employees ...' A text issued in 1961 by Bishop Custodio Alvin Pereira, who was then auxiliary bishop of Lourenco Marques illustrates the type of unacknowledged political bias which resulted in Mozambique: Bishop Pereira distinguished nine principles of action consequent on the Concordat:

1. Independence, in itself, is something indifferent to the welfare of man. It can be a good thing when certain geographical and cultural conditions are verified.

2. Until such conditions are verified, to want to take the part of independence movements is an act contrary to nature.

3. Even when the necessary conditions are verified, the Motherland has the right to withhold independence, if freedoms and rights are respected, and general welfare, civil and religious progress are all being pursued.

4. All movements that resort to force are contrary to the natural law, even when independence is a good thing, it must be obtained by peaceful means.

5. As to terrorist movements, the clergy has the obligation, not only to distance itself from them, but to oppose them. This is a logical conclusion from their very mission.

6. When such a movement is non-violent, it is fitting that the clergy distance itself from it: theirs is a spiritual mission. Superiors can impose such a distancing: in Lourenco Marques it is in fact imposed.

7. The native peoples in Africa have a debt of gratitude to the colonizing peoples, for all the benefits received from them.

8. Educated persons have the obligation of disillusioning less educated persons as to the false image of independence.

9. Practically all African independence movements are stigmatized by the sign of revolt and communism; such movements cannot, therefore, be approved of. The teaching of the Holy See is altogether clear on atheistic and revolutionary communism. The great revolution is the gospel.

How can we make amends for the way in which the church continues to act as the dupe of secular powers for the destruction of human life? Mention of the red menace still makes grown up people into children. The Roman Catholic Church in Chile was something of a model for the rest of that continent. It not only spoke words of compassion on behalf of the poor but sold its property to give to them. In Allende, it had as chief of state an incredibly constitutionalist Marxist. Yet, when the crunch came, it played its part in illustrating the classical Marxist thesis that, unless the internal interests which ally themselves with external imperialistic powers are dealt with, unless the church is put in its place, unless the military machine is controlled, no revolution of the people can succeed. In the end the landed, property-owning, affluent and middle classes teamed up with the military and used the 'neutrality' of the church to undermine and overthrow a constitutional régime.

Did the church really want to be a partner in the violence which was unleashed – which was clearly not directed at those who were promoting disorder in the state (since, for instance, none of the lorry drivers and their firms were called to account)? Did it really want to be party to the hounding, torture and bloody elimination of people just because they were coming alive to the promise of a new order of society?

Did the church intentionally condone the pressures brought on legitimate government by international combines like the ITT, the hostile policies of foreign governments (the USA withdrew finance – except that which went to the building up of the army!), the loaded operations of banks – so that chaos was caused in a society starved of money, which could then be ascribed to left-wing mismanagement?

Did the church really want to see children, who under Allende got ten times the amount of milk they had ever enjoyed previously, going back to their starvation rations? Did it want to see people who were getting enough to eat at last, with empty bellies?

Did the church want to see human beings losing the spark of vitality and aspiration which the hope of a better society held out to them?

Did the church long for an end to the traditional neutrality of the army, and the establishment of a totalitarian régime in place of democracy?

Whatever the church might have wanted to do, it was how it acted that counted. One year on, it is virtually the only force in the land to stand between the dictatorship and the people, shielding, succouring, providing means of escape. But must the church's courage always be shown in picking up the bits?

A leading Marxist in Kerala was asked what he felt about the church. If the Communists should not only come to power but stay in power in that country, would it not prove to be an awkward obstacle, a stumbling block in the path of the policies a Marxist government would develop? 'Not at all', replied the Communist leader, 'once we are in power, the church will quickly change its tune. It always does. In no time at all it will find good theological reasons for working with us. The church is no problem.'

The charismatic General Secretary of the Communist Party in Le Réunion, the island in the Indian Ocean, saw the captivity of the church, but understood it in a more positive light. The church, he said, will never be able to act in freedom and give what it really has to give people, according to its message, until there is a change of power. French colonialist influence must go. Once that happens, the church will have a chance to become itself, instead of fitting in with an oppressive system. Something similar is being said in many parts of Latin America. The church as an institutional body has become so conformed to the secular powers-that-be that it has no hope of breaking clear except through a process of political change which breaks the grip of the old system.

And so the church in the world is desperately weak with the wrong kind of weakness. It is not weak like Jesus, facing up to the secular and religious authorities in the crisis of his life, and ending up on a cross. It is weak in its self-interest, and in the capacity of secular powers to use that self-interest to hoodwink it, time after time, into persuading itself that it also protects God's interests if it protects their interests. It must now lose its life, politically, to find it, instead of saving its life, politically, and letting men die.

## A Change of Course

One can only speak of contrary and contradictory signs in the life of the church. But one can certainly say, with good grounds for doing so, that while there is plenty of evidence of the church's continuing tie-up with every type of *status quo*, there is fresh evidence of a change in the 'patron' relationships both to the poor and to the powers-that-be. Formative forces at work have been the shake-up of the last World War; the development of media of communication[9] so that all kinds of people who were out of touch are in touch with what is happening in the world; and the re-evaluation of the church's life which has been made possible by the existence of a World Council of Churches and the event of Vatican II. The direction of life is no longer as it was.

One cannot be long among the awakened poor of Latin America before one hears the contrast between things done *'de arriba'* and *'de bajo'*. *'De arriba'* speaks of movement from the top, where consultation takes place and decisions are made, down, where people are told what is good for them and are called upon to implement decisions made for them. *'De bajo'* speaks of springs of life from below which touch the roots of humanity so that creative forces can sprout and flourish in a whole variety of ways. Things which come *'de arriba'* leave people lifeless. Things which come *'de bajo'* bring people alive. The choice of the *'de bajo'* form of operation is profoundly biblical. God the Creator forms man as a creative being. Jesus Christ the Son inserts himself into the human situation, in fullest identification with others, to bring new life there. The Spirit awakens human beings to take a lively part in the whole work of God from where they are. The words for 'life' in the New Testament have to do with the awakening of an inner dynamic in human beings, not with some capacity for movement transferred from 'somewhere up there'. The gospel releases people to be their lively selves, with all the risks that that entails. But the way of all kinds of authorities, including church authorities, seems to be incurably *'de arriba'*.

In a *barrio* in San José, Costa Rica, some hundreds of people had invaded land and built their shanties on either side of a small polluted stream. The local authority had stepped in, and a housing scheme with far superior accommodation was being completed for them nearby. None of those to whom I spoke wanted to move to it. 'We had no say in the building of the scheme. It is not the way we would plan it,' was their sufficient comment.

A new project for housing gipsies near London, beautifully designed on paper, was lacking in the basic things which would have been built in if gipsies themselves had been asked to share in designing their community – means of bringing unsorted scrap metal under their window through the night; provision for the many members of an extended family to live near one another; provision for animals, very much a part of a gipsy's life. Some caravans were so placed that the owners could not even move in or out if neighbours on either side were absent.

This contrasted sharply with the way in which slumdwellers in Nochinagar, Madras, India, moved recently to simple three-storey flats. There was consultation with the community at every point. Changes in plan were negotiated – for instance those who wanted to be near relatives and neighbours were located accordingly. People were given fifty rupees each to demolish their huts, and sufficient palm leaves to establish other dwellings around the building site – thus allowing them to rebuild an interim community with the leadership intact, and at the same time to keep an eagle eye on the construction work. Chickens and water buffalo stayed around the houses. The motto of the board responsible is for once appropriate: 'We shall see God in the smile of the poor.'

It is a simple fact, which experts find incredibly difficult to grasp, that community is made 'de bajo'. People know how to make community. Planners can help by offering auxiliary skills. 'Want to see how people really make community?' asked a youth worker in Zambia – and he took me to an illegal township where buildings were made of anything available but where there was real neighbourliness in the arrangement of dwellings. The young slum dweller in Caracas, Venezuela, whose wife looked already old as she nursed her first child, was asked: 'Why wouldn't you live in the housing scheme over there provided by the government?' 'Because,' he said, 'we could not afford the rent; we like animals around us and they are forbidden; here people are always ready to lend a helping hand whereas there you would be on your own.' El Salvador is a city in itself, just outside Lima, Peru, created by the invasion of the landless. As was noted earlier, they made broad avenues and left wide spaces for community development. They knew what they wanted. Sympathetic student helpers who had planning and architectural skills, helped them to realize their design. The people's skills were for living life-in-community. The students' skills were auxiliary aids. Each respected the other, and true proportion was kept.

One sign of hope is that the church, often in ecumenical teams, is operating much more 'de bajo', getting alongside people instead of trying to govern their lives from above.

Blind workers are particularly exploitable, both economically and spiritually. A work-force of blind people in Hong Kong felt driven to the point where they had to do something more drastic about their situation than just protest verbally to the management. They lacked job security. Their wages were low. The administration seemed to them to be unsympathetic. A change of policy was under consideration which could make the workshop operate on a more impersonal basis. They went on strike, and turned to an ecumenical team for support. The Hong Kong Christian Industrial Committee placed before the public, through its *Workers' Weekly*, the facts which other papers would not publish. Representatives from that Committee and Roman Catholics – who had been the first to act – formed a support group.

The temptation to take over the situation must have been strong. Blind people have a look of helplessness: and the sighted may forget that they have all their wits about them. But this worked out as an 'alongside' operation. The initiative was left with the blind workers. They decided to march the streets to bring the attention of the public to their cause – the support group simply saw to it that they kept clear of traffic. They decided to hold a sit-in: the support group enabled them to carry through their decision, taking in blankets and food, leading people to the toilet, etc. About 200 took up strategic stances, sleeping out at the Star Ferry, and raised $50,000 (Hong Kong) for a fighting fund: the support team helped them to find the right kind of lawyer.

To be present at a meeting of the Strategic Planning Committee was to realize the new vitality possessed by the blind workers, helped by an awareness that, backed up by others, they could fight their own battles and fight them successfully. One leader in particular had a very acute grasp of the theological issues at stake. They won through and are now helping a more militant form of organization to develop among all the blind workers of Hong Kong.

A community of street hawkers in Hong Kong who suffered from police harassment and the pressures of the commercial community, had this to say, as non-Christians, of the work of a similar team which gave them support and spoke up for them in court: 'They give the poor some hope and strength.'

Nima is a community swollen by immigration until it is bursting at the seams. It is on the fringe of Accra, Ghana, a country which, because of its relative wealth, attracts people from surrounding, poorer territories. Into Nima crowded people of many languages, looking for work and habitation – from Togo, Dahoméy, Upper Volta, Mali and Guinea. The pressure became too great. Essential services collapsed. The government gave up. The people threw in their hand. Nobody quite knew what to do with the problem area. Refuse mounted. Sanitation broke down. The place became more and more of a slum.

Then the government made known a plan to relocate all the inhabitants, and clear the whole area by straight demolition. A group of students, including James Sarpei, realized that this would simply create another Nima elsewhere. So they moved in. They spent most of their time clearing up the area, removing filthy-smelling refuse. People around became interested. They joined in. As they saw that the situation could be improved by their own efforts, they took heart. Students and local people began to talk together to share problems and hopes to confide in one another.

From this, a new spirit developed. The right kind of trusted leadership came forward. Apathy gave way to the flowering of community initiative. The people built a community centre for themselves. Under Dr Busia's centralized form of government, the building was taken over, and the people lost heart. But now they have fresh encouragement from the government, and have appointed two developmental welfare committees to work with the high-powered, top-level government Committee for the Redevelopment of Nima and Malubi. The ministry of the Christian group has been to help to co-ordinate the efforts of the people and suggest how these might be most effective.

A gauge of the sensitiveness of the approach of the Christian team is illustrated by the good relationships which obtain with Moslems. The latter are fully engaged in the total work, feel they are respected, and know that when they enter into dialogue about the deep things of life they will not be manoeuvered on to ground which will set them at a disadvantage.

Pastor Ayadji, a member of the Apostolic Action Team working in the Fon area of Dahoméy, had a difficult choice to make when he became a Christian. He belonged to a community whose religion was animist. They set great store on respect paid to ancestors, and on rites fulfilled to acknowledge their presence and authority. He could have left the region; and his people would have welcomed such a choice, because it would have got rid of an embarrassment. But if he had done so, there would be no Christian witness in their midst – and to that he felt called from the beginning of his new life. He knew that if he stayed there would be attempts to poison him – he would be thought of as a spot of cancer in the body which would infect the whole if it were not got rid of. He knew that to stay meant to take part in ancestor rites. But this he felt he could do, since ancestors are not thought of as gods but more as super-human beings who have powers to favour or disfavour the living, who need to be kept informed and consulted about every development in the community's life. He stayed. He offered sacrifices. He kept vigilant, in case of poisoning attempts.

A harder decision awaited him. His young son was chosen to go to a fetish-teacher's school for training. If the father refused, the boy would become the object of resentment and would be much more likely to succumb to poisoning attempts. The pastor argued 'If the power of God has shielded me in all my life in this community, will it not also shield the boy?' He let him go.

And so he has won respect and understanding for a faith which must have seemed at first to be one which would cut an African community from its own indigenous roots and its own valued practices. He stayed in. So he was listened to. He gained much which has helped him in his wider ministry in the Fon area from those who at one time wanted nothing so much as to get rid of him.

There are signs of change of course also at a different level. It is no longer strange to see pastors, priests, nuns and deacons in acts of protest and opposition to government on specific issues. They have been expelled in droves in these last years from countries of Southern Africa wherever they have tried to stand up for the rights of the people. In Panama, Father Hector Gallego, disappearing from sight with a scream and leaving behind him a trail of blood, has proved to be a martyr who has stimulated others to fight injustice and oppression. In Korea more and more Protestant pastors and laymen are in prison for speaking out for freedom. Part of the problem of the military coup in Chile was the danger it represented to pastors and priests from other Latin American countries who had taken refuge there as wanted men. There has been the suicide of two leaders of the Presbyterian Church in Mozambique – including the church president – as the result of isolation and severe interrogation in jail at the end of 1972. Events like these are straws in the wind. True, publicity tends to be given only when the ordained are ill-treated, and it has nearly always been lay people who have borne the brunt of being pioneers of new life. But since the oppressiveness of the past can be ascribed particularly to the ordained – to hierarchies and church bureaucracies – it is at that level that an alteration of course can be more clearly discerned. Something new is happening.

The need for repentance is being seen in a more total and realistic perspective. A statement signed by eighteen Roman Catholic bishops and major religious superiors of the North-east of Brazil, issued on 6 May 1973, includes the following:

We have to recognize in a spirit of true humility and penance that the Church has not always been faithful to its prophetic mission, to its evangelical role of being at the side of the people. How many times, involved in the mesh of evils existing in this world, the Church, under deceitful disguises, whether due to ingenuousness or captiousness, in a sad deformation of the evangelical message, has played the game of the oppressors and received favors from those who hold the power of money and of politics against the common good? But at each hour of its existence the Word of God is sent to the Church and invites it to repent, to be converted, to return to its 'fervor of the first days' (Rev. 2.4).

Particular churches are not only learning to recognize the sins of their past but also to confess them publicly. Among ten theses on the Rhenish Mission in the former German South West Africa, 1880–1914/1918, issued by the president of the Evangelical Lutheran Church in Namibia, 11 March 1971, one finds these:

5. German colonialism in South West Africa was characterized by cruelty, exploitation and oppression, which exposes the myth of the 'good old German times' as a lie. South African despotism has simply taken over this heritage of blood and shame, and it has been kept up to our own time.

6. The Rhenish Mission Society, with its missionaries, was in the middle of this whirl: as pioneers of colonialism, partners at the concluding of the so-called protective treaties, advisers in the execution of colonial projects.

7. The failure of the mission during the political crisis in South West Africa could be imputed to a non-biblical understanding of neutrality and patriotism, as well as to misinterpretations of Martin Luther's doctrine on the two kingdoms.

8. The twofold loyalty the missionaries maintain with regard to both the colonial authorities and their African communities has caused a tragedy, which has cast long shadows on the ecclesiastical history of South West Africa.

9. At the most critical moments, the mission has often been guilty of silence; this has not only made it an accomplice of various crimes and murders, but first and foremost it has also shaken the confidence of the missionary communities in South West Africa. Whether this confidence will be totally restored remains to be seen. It is a grace of God that the mission has been able to continue its activity in South West Africa after the colonial period.

10. In these days of neo-colonialism under South African despotism, the mission and the churches confront the same problem as they did during the German colonial period. Church and mission in South West Africa must examine whether for the white and non-white populations of South and South West Africa they really bear witness to the Gospel in its entirety.

The 1971 International Theological Conference on Evangelization and Dialogue in India was one of many congresses which was explicit about the need for the engagement of the church in politics. The 35th point of its final declaration reads:

Today politics is an important area for the realization of the values of the Kingdom of God, such as social justice, human brotherhood and human dignity. Christians, therefore, must participate with others in political action to bring about urgently required social reforms.

Priests and religious too cannot remain indifferent to these issues when fundamental problems of justice are involved. The example of several of our missionaries who had the courage to stand up for the rights of a powerless and defenceless people should be an inspiration to us. In future the animation of the laity in this field may involve many more priests and religious in the risks of such struggles for justice. In such situations they will need the understanding, sympathy and support of their brother priests and religious communities.

Although Christians are co-operating with many men of goodwill, there is no sellout, as movements in the heart of South America and in the Indian Ocean illustrate.

Among the campesinos of Paraguay you will find a movement of the Spirit manifested in groups which do not depend on the hierarchy but which remain an integral part of the life of the church. Courses on Marxism are used to clarify their understanding of how society works. Priests or trained laity lead groups, scattered all through the rural areas, in Bible study. Marxists are puzzled that they cannot capture the hearts and minds of these peasants, for they accept their tools and reject their overall philosophy.

A small group of Témoinage Chrétien on the Isle of Réunion in the Indian Ocean chose to insert themselves entirely in the Communist party's anti-colonialist struggle – for that, they believed, represented the clearest claim on their obedience and the first priority for action. The visit of a World Council of Churches representative and one of their own headquarters staff gave them pause to think. At a communion service conducted jointly by a Dominican priest and a Church of Scotland pastor, they asked to lead in confession. There they affirmed their conviction about the rightness of their basic choice; but confessed their failure to contribute theological perspectives on the struggle in which they were engaged, promising to amend that matter in the future.

An underground movement of people of many denominations in the Philippines, face the options before Christians in that country starkly. A statement they issued recently includes the following:

1. If we are mainly concerned for ourselves, to preserve our status and present activities (apostolate, schools, social work, catechetical and liturgical activities), believing these are for the people, then we will have to seek accommodation with the present dispensation. It is unrealistic to expect the authorities of the church to go underground.

2. If we are for the liberation of the broad majority, then we have to accept the discipline and penance of the struggle. Pilgrims with lighter

packs. Fewer responsibilities, that enable us to respond without vacillation and hesitation. To be able to respond to the people's call, we should not feel responsible for so many structures, not even for new structures and the movement of liberation.

The concreteness of the choices being made may be finally indicated by the report of the Peruvian Episcopate contributed to the 1971 Synod of Bishops in Rome:

On behalf of those who 'have no voice', but who silently suffer the most inhuman consequences of a system of domination and exploitation caused by the centers of power (economic, political, scientific, etc.), both intra- and extra-national, which decide the fate of the peoples in unequal and unjust competition, we wish to act as loud-speakers for the protest of numerous tribes in the Peruvian Amazon region, who cry out desperately in languages which the 'civilized and/or Christian people' will not or cannot understand:

We are men and we are entitled to be recognized as such, and therefore we demand the legal personality which as persons and as a group we are still being denied.

We are entitled to the land on which we have lived since time immemorial, where we were born and where we bury our elders, and therefore we demand the legal ownership which is still being denied us.

We are entitled to life, and therefore we demand that we be permitted to survive and to live in a dignified manner.

We are entitled to be different, and therefore we demand to be respected as persons and groups, which at present is denied us.

We are entitled to form part of the Peruvian nation without being enslaved, and therefore we demand autonomy, equality and freedom, which so far have been denied us.

These cries are the expression of a situation of injustice which violates man's most fundamental rights and which attacks the cultural and even the biological survival of numerous ethnic groups.

Before such injustice, the Church, through her Apostolic Vicariates entrusted with the responsibility of announcing and fulfilling Christian justice:

(*a*) Reaffirms the human reality of the native and the utmost respect for his culture.

(*b*) Considers it her basic obligation, as the Church, to discover, know and appreciate the values of these ethnic groups which show the presence of God and of Christ incarnate in their history.

(*c*) Is convinced she has the primordial duty of achieving justice among the natives, as the sole basis for the truth, love and peace of the Good News: Christ.

Therefore the Peruvian Church sternly condemns and seriously undertakes to wield all its influence to bring about substantial changes with respect to:

(*a*) The present legal defenselessness of the great majority of natives in the Peruvian Amazon legislation or documents as citizens.

(*b*) The invasion, relocation and systematic expropriation of lands inhabited by the natives since time immemorial, since the great majority are totally lacking any legal deed of ownership.

(*c*) The vexations and injustices (rarely sanctioned) suffered by the natives through abuse of authority, deceit, theft, and further inhuman exploitation.

(*d*) The insufficient health attention, both preventive and curative, suffered by the natives faced with biological disintegration, caused or heightened by their contacts with the national community.

The omens point to a harder time for dictatorships and olig-archies of the right and of the left. The church is not so likely to be fitted into the designs of powers-that-be. Even hierarchies, those least flexible and least representative parts of the church, are no longer the soft mark they were. The fire runs.

But the basic problem may remain. May not the church be simply fitting in shrewdly with alternative secular forces when it takes the side of the oppressed today?

It is testified throughout the Bible that God is not even and equal in his judgments – as in the figure of Justice, blindfolded, with balanced scales. God is heavily biased on the side of the poor. To be on the side of the poor is a sign of awareness of God's purpose. All other forms of taking sides must be brought to the bar of this basic commitment.

But how is a distinctive Christian witness to be maintained in the consequent struggles?

In answer, one may share four perceptions which seem to be deep-rooted in a church growing to maturity in many parts of the world.

1. The distinctiveness of the Christian witness may not be some-thing which is all that important. When Jesus Christ became man he emptied himself, among other things, of the security of being distinctive. He was hidden in the flow of human life. He advocated doing the right, even if that were quite misinterpreted, and his followers were reviled for it. If we are too keen to label our actions especially, we may be concentrating too much on ourselves, when we should allow the actions to point away from us. We need to be reminded again of the saying: 'Let your light so shine before men that they may see your good works *and glorify your Father who is in heaven.*'

2. What is essential is commitment. The Christian is not to stand on the sidelines waiting for the perfect situation to develop before he risks his faith in embroilment. Testing his actions con-tinually with fellow-Christians of all kinds, ready to change the manner of his involvement as new light comes, he will find only one place of response to God and of illumination – the thick of the fight. In relation to the battle, he will have a specific calling and

will know when to stand aside, when to risk everything, what to do and say and suffer. The Spirit will tell him.

3. The commitment will place the struggle to which he must give his whole heart within the context of the struggle in which man engages with God for a new world. So the Christian will have this difficult task to fulfill when he takes sides – he will bring to his other comrades-in-arms a larger vision. The effect will be to check the natural human tendency to transform wars-which-have-to-be-fought into holy wars, and enemies into dismissable caricatures (how powerful a hate-weapon the cartoon is in wartime!). This does not represent a withdrawal, or a limitation of commitment. Rather it is a gift to the side he takes – hard to offer and hard to receive – which will allow the struggle to be seen in a more all-embracing context and will counter tendencies to fanaticism.

4. Finally, there is a conviction that life moves towards a D-day when everything will come to a head. This implies two kinds of hard work for Christians: preparation, and waiting and discernment.

The final prayer is that God's kingdom may come, the success of any particular revolution being only contributory to that final end. The final acknowledgment is that kingdom, power and glory are not mankind's but God's. Human beings can live with hope because God's way of working the world will be realized. But all through history God comes to meet mankind's striving, and prepares opportunities for the partial realization of what will be finally fulfilled in its completeness. One finds this awareness in several parts of Latin America in talk of a 'Day' for which people must 'have respect'; and in Asia in talk of 'firewood' and 'sparks'.

Talk of the 'Day' relates to situations where people do not have power at the moment, or believe they should not take power at the moment, but who anticipate a decisive hour in the future for which they must be ready. In contradiction to those who see no further than a particular revolution they are not clear what will be asked of them – to throw life away, or husband it, to go with the revolutionary tide or stand against it, to be crowned or crucified. The Day will reveal it. Meantime, they must take pains to be ready. They must be praying, politically acute, instructed, lively and critical disciples. The Day must find them ready.

Talk of the 'firewood' and 'sparks' relates to groups in struggle who believe they must 'gather firewood', leaving the 'spark which will catch everything alight' to come from outside men's contriving. Their job is to make sure that the firewood is there – they must work to get everything ready. The spark will be something they cannot programme and must not strike. Through some event or pressure or word which may seem quite insignificant in itself,

God will provide the spark. If his people have done their bit, the fire will take.

What signs are there in the churches of the West that they are equipping themselves for a Day of the Lord or gathering firewood for God's decisive spark? Will not the Day come upon them like a thief? Will not the spark fall to the ground?

## 2 An End to Theological Tribalism

In early May 1973 a company of professional theologians, journalists and other laymen gathered at the Ecumenical Centre, Geneva. They were prepared to expose themselves to theological insights offered by Black Theology (James H. Cone from the USA and Eduardo J. Bodipo-Malumba from Equatorial Guinea) and Latin American Theology of Liberation (Hugo Assmann from Chile and Paulo Freire from Brazil). The initiative came from the working group on Renewal and Renewal Movements in the Unit of Education and Renewal of the WCC.

The main result was non-meeting, non-communication and bewilderment all round.

'What is all this?' you might hear a small group asking itself over coffee, 'What are they saying? Nothing clear is coming through to us that seems to be all that important. Was it for as little as this that we laid aside five days of precious time?' 'What is really fresh in this material?' the next group might be asking, 'Exodus is given star billing. In one case the Great Oppressor, the Pharaoh, is identified as racialism; in the other capitalism. But none of that is new. Is all this stuff meant to be radically different?'

What many seem to have expected was a contribution which would directly challenge and nourish their own thinking, meeting them where they were. They were disoriented to find they were being asked instead to enter into a different world. It was all the more confusing that it appeared to be an Alice in Wonderland world. 'Things which seem oversimple', they were told, 'may be profound: listen again. Things which seem disconnected may have subtle connections: look again. The main thing we may have to say is that we can't say much here, except – how engaged are you in the struggle for a new world, brother? Only in that struggle can theology come alive. Only when you and we are deep in that struggle can we begin to understand one another.'

If what was presented could have been reduced to words and concepts which the Europeans could handle comfortably, what would have been the upshot? At most, a fresh excitement for jaded theological and journalistic palates. People would have been left right where they were.

The first main point made by Hugo Assmann after he had stated the purpose of his presentation should have clarified the situation, had it been heard. The Theology of Liberation, he said, had been blown up to mythical proportions. That came from dissociating *statements* ('texts') from the *action* ('praxis') with which they were interwoven: 'In the consideration of texts, which are nearly always provisional and circumstantial, the analysis does not include the praxis and its situational context – which gave rise to these texts *as historical instruments of struggle*.[10] Thus, what appears in the writings as an essential reference of origin and finality, praxis, passes once again to a secondary level.' He then goes on to speak of the 'draining of new languages' which this implies and points out that

... the same languages can mean things which are historically in conflict. This conclusion, so simple in itself, has tremendous consequences for those of us who are convinced that faith is necessarily something concrete, at a level of political praxis.

And he goes on about testimonies made from the heart of the struggle

... when much more relevant things happen in the life of the people than are happening (or rather 'not happening') in theology, it is a good sign that the testimonies – fragmentary, provisory, without much abstract theoretical consistency – have a theological resonance greater than that of theological treatises.

Perhaps what is positive about the enormous repercussion of our Christian babbling in Latin America is precisely in this point: its testimonial character from the heart of a decided struggle against Capitalist oppression. If this is what has awakened a certain interest, it is good to follow along this line. This means: don't take our writings for something which they are not (pure abstract theorising); don't transform us into something to be consumed, to make up for any sort of impotence on your part; don't be spectators of the little we achieve, nor project on to Latin America an image of compensations; finally, enter with decision, each in his own context, the same struggle ...

James Cone began his address as follows:

Since the appearance of 'Black Theology' in North America, 'Liberation Theology' in Latin America and 'Political Theology' in many countries, it is no longer possible to do Christian Theology without taking seriously the question of freedom in history for the hope of mankind. The black struggle for liberation in history is related to oppressed peoples' struggle for liberation throughout the whole world, and forces Christian theology to ask: what is freedom and how is it related to oppressed peoples striving for a humane future?[11]

As the four protagonists spoke and argued there were intimations of threat in the air. But who or what was threatened? What was all this non-meeting about?

What is threatened in such meeting is the basic assumption of a part of the world which has dominated theological thinking for centuries, that its interests, priorities, methods and quality of scholarship provide a universal norm. 'Anything which is relevant to theological debate, can be translated into a language we understand, and be spoken to us so that we can hear it where we are', its protagonists might almost be heard to say.

Note that it is taken for granted:

(*a*) that 'where we are' is important for humanity; (*b*) that our way of doing theology is universally valid and acceptable; (*c*) that clear and systematic thinking is possible when you are in the thick of a confused liberation struggle; (*d*) that communication with those who have traditionally held the theological ring is essential, and a means of gauging whether you and others are on the right lines or not!

At the meeting of the Central Committee in Rochester, USA in 1963, Mr M'Timkulu, who was then Director of the Mindolo Ecumenical Foundation was asked, in conversation, how Africans responded to the threat posed to the world by nuclear weapons. 'We don't give it much thought', he replied. 'But surely that is the crucial threat posed to the whole of humanity today!' 'It may seem to be so to you in Europe. We in Zambia have more important things to take up our energies at this point of history.' His questioner went away shaking his head. How could Africans be so out of touch with the real life-and-death issues when they were so obvious to Europeans?

It is still not sinking in. When the Northern Hemisphere plays its favourite theological and political tunes, the rest of the world will no longer dance. In fact, the rest of the world is not even likely to listen – it is more likely to be elsewhere doing things it considers more important.

We are in a new situation.

1. The Euro-American traditions which had dominated for so long are no longer taken as points of departure – far less as reference points for checking on the validity and quality of other theologies. The need for disengagement from them is felt often more keenly than the need for engagement.[12] But for this new firmness and independence, insights growing and developing in other parts of the world would still be being thought of as, at

best, raw materials for manufacture on the same old traditional premises. One thing above all must preoccupy those who are concerned that new theological testimony from their geographical region should make impact with its own identity and in all its integrity: the old systems must be denied the opportunity to assimilate the new life into their blood-stream in order to revitalize themselves. From now on, contributions from Europe and America must be treated simply as contributions among others. They are not to be despised in their turn. But they cannot present themselves convincingly any longer as theologically normative. An Amerindian writes:

If we have Bibles and Communion why do we need doctrine conceived in another civilization? Why should we need Augustine, Aquinas, Barth and Tillich when in our past we have Beganawidah, Tecumseh, Quetzalcoatl and Chilan Balan?

2. The strong assertion is made that theology emerges basically from struggle – not from study. Those who discern how God is at work in the world will be those concretely committed to participating with him in the work of transforming it into the world of his promise. You can't do theology from the sidelines. Yes, reflection is needed, in interplay with action. Yes, books are needed to set strivings and perceptions at this point of history and in any one part of the world into the perspective of God's work through history and to the ends of the earth. But the place of illumination is the thick of the fight.

One can *feel* the anger of Asians and Latin Americans – those who think it worth more than a resigned shrug of the shoulders – at the Moltmanns of this world, who theologize on revolution from detached, academic positions. A detached position in theology is a disqualification for doing theology. Words which are disrelated from experience and commitment, as the very terminology of the Bible should make clear, are fraudulent though they deceive the very elect. The new possibilities God introduces into history may be turned by words into opportunities for adventurous journeys of the mind without leaving home. This is nothing other than sinful diversion, when the professional theologian of the West has quite clear vocations:

There is the sadly neglected vocation to silence.

There is the vocation to leave academic surroundings and take Abrahamic risks in unfamiliar community with people.

There is the calling to listen sensitively in the communion of saints to the discoveries others are making as they participate in the revolutionary ferment God is creating in so many places – not to interpret these (which often means emasculating them) but to point to them and instruct the ears and eyes of others to new ranges of hearing and sight.

There is a share in the immense task of conversion, of changing attitudes, values and priorities in the Northern Hemisphere, so that these changes are seen to be commanded by God.

3. It is being made clearer than ever before that theologies are inextricably bound up with histories. Why did theological traditions of the West dominate for so long? Because of their quality? They belonged to a flow of dominating history. They adopted for themselves a prestige status because they were part of a history which asserted for itself a prestige status. The histories of the Western world have imposed themselves on other histories, eliminating, domesticating, distorting them. Now that people are freeing themselves to recover histories which had been despised and set aside, and also to forge their own histories in this decisive time, they inevitably set their hand to create relevant theologies. To regain one's own history is to recover a base for one's own theology. It is to achieve a specific theological identity; and at the same time to develop a basis for making a distinctive contribution to world theology.

4. It is being made clear that words are too deceptive a currency for interpretation of other minds and lives. They can conceal not only nuances and overtones which are simply not translatable: they may draw the whole sting out of alternative ways of living and thinking. The temptation always is to load our familiar cart with sheaves of new words.

In ecumenical and other circles, words are often worn out before they have done their work deeply in the consciousness of the Christian community – word-pedlars handle them until they have removed the fresh sheen of excitement, and then drop them for other ones which are promisingly strange and new.

In this situation it has seemed to some who are concerned with alternative theologies, that the only constructive recourse is to make words a barrier to understanding, instead of a bridge. If words are heard and understood by you where you are, you are encouraged to stay where and as you are. But if the invitation is to listen to a different history, really to expose yourself to that history and take seriously the changes-towards-righteous-relationship implied for your part of the world, you must move. It can be redemptive that words will make sense, if they are heard in a foreign, authentic context, only if we move our ground elsewhere, where they can be respected and understood.

5. But Black, Latin American and Asian theologies hold out a bigger threat and a more ample promise. They are not only a breach in the Western wall. They are the first trickle of a great flood. They are the beginning of the assertion by all peoples that

their histories, cultures and mythologies offer means for theological perception which are as valid as any. In the rise of previously dominated peoples, the tribalism of Western theology is ready to be swept away.

Until recently it had been held that there is a universal body of theological knowledge of which the West is the trustee – and that other parts of the world, once they approach the same maturity, can add to this body and enrich it. We have been made to see that what was treated as universal is merely tribalistic. We are, dangerously, at the beginning of world theology. There can no longer be a monarchy, only a commonwealth.

## Re-inheriting the Theological Community

Theology is returning to the hands of the true 'makers'.[13]

New theologies which crack open Western dominance are still mainly being promoted by professional theologians. Theology has not only been marked by historical and cultural dominations. It has also suffered from domination by professionals. It has been monopolized by those equipped with certain kinds of scholarly skills. Their training, as it qualifies for certain kinds of work, disqualifies for other theological work. Professionals have acted as if the whole range of theology were their own battlefield. In fact they are mainly campfollowers providing supplies for the main force, auxiliaries checking on the efficiency of its weapons.

The people of God themselves are the theological community. In their struggle to transform the world, they perceive how and where God is at work and what kind of God he is revealing himself to be. Not only are their perceptions crucial: nothing less than the whole living and breathing Christian community possesses the variety of experience and insight to provide adequate testimony to God's work today. A basic language underlies this basic struggle, a language of discovery and suffering.

So often theology has been a Babel, estranging parts of the Christian community from others by thought-and-speech-barriers – by jargon, by concepts treated as if they had universal currency which have only limited acceptance. The language of discovery and suffering in the kingdom of Christ communicates everywhere. Live for even a short time with a deprived group; marvel at their concern for the establishing of righteousness; marvel at the fierce joy they know under the pressures of poverty and police. Give time to enter into the situation and let it make its impact.[14] Then share with them what seems relevant for the life of that Christian community from brothers in other parts of the world. They are immediately on the wavelength of Filipinos, Koreans, Malagasys,

Ugandans, Chileans, Bolivians. The language of common life, drawn from vivid participation in history as servants of the living God, provides the only credible and effective instrument for the basic work of theology.[15]

Theology in the Bible is rarely a sophisticated web of thought which only the specially educated can follow. It is poetry and drama, jewelled sayings in which succeeding centuries discover new fires; parable, story, disturbing question, with no answer attached. By some equivalent of cultural shame, common people have been taught to downgrade their own insights and contributions – when, in fact, their theology has this basic biblical character.

The theological thinking of common people is often in germ form – but so is the most compelling poetry. It is expressed in stories and riddles rather than theses – what that means is that it is more totally integrated into life than is abstract thinking. Common peoples' thinking on God can no more be treated as 'pre-theological' than a poem can be called pretestimonial when compared with a doctoral thesis written on it.

But it is different – more direct in perception, more immediately related to living out the faith in concrete situations.

Theology is a life-risk. Admittedly, by nature it requires a certain withdrawal from the full stream of life to gain perspective. For it demands that the best resources of the mind be brought to bear – to probe, check, compare, set out and test conclusions. But theological thinking remains part of a total response to God. Bare the humble enquiring mind to him and you expose the whole being of an individual or group. You risk all that may happen in that encounter. So any theological enterprise should naturally show a tendency to spill over into experiences of conviction of sin, repentence, conversion, new freedom, new self-offering, the forging of new community across old dividing lines. Faces will light up with a new radiance, bodies become vibrant, faith burst forth in agonized groaning, praise, song, prayer, poetry, litanies, messianic feasting. Set your hand to theology and you risk all that may happen through living contact with the Trinity.

What was lacking when theology was treated as a limited activity for people with a particular equipment is restored in those crucial encounters in which the whole church is re-discovering itself as a theological community.

Here is a case in point. Sra Valenzuela from Chile, editor of the New Life in Christ Course (well-known in Latin America as an all-age education project) was interviewed in Lima, Peru. She had just spent ten days running a Writers' Workshop for the course on the theme 'New Heavens and New Earth'. Taking part were a journalist, students including a sociologist, teachers, a pastor and

a woman deacon. Some were radicals, others came from very conservative church backgrounds. They represented a wide range of
traditions – Roman Catholic, Methodist, Lutheran, National
Peruvian Church and Christian Missionary Alliance.

Q. What is your approach in these Writers' Workshops?

A. I feel that people must grapple with the word of God, and I
say to them, 'You must stay with this biblical passage until it
speaks to you as a person, until you have a real encounter with this
word of God. Only then will you be able to write'. I find that as
people reflect upon their own life situations in the light of a passage
of scripture their whole life is illuminated. Their personal experience speaks to the text and the text speaks back. So God's word
comes alive for them. Then they can write; but not before.

A second important thing is that when people make discoveries
and take time to realize the significance of the new things they
begin to see, they must share these with the group. The final product is the fruit of a process of group dynamics. Discoveries need to
be tested in the wider group and criteria for the writing of the
publication worked out – otherwise what is said may be too individual and subjective.

Q. Do pastors tend to dominate the discussions?

A. Unfortunately the pastors are often the ones who least understand what we are looking for. Every pastor in every workshop that
I have ever worked in first brings me a sermon. I try to say to him,
'I am not interested in your preaching to me. I want you to open
the word of God to me in such a way that I may see my life in
the light of that passage. If you try to tell me all the answers, I
will never see my life, for I won't have to think, you'll have told
me it all.' I have watched men and women, pastors who have had
a high theological training in seminaries, struggle to forget that
they have to give the answers. They also tend to think too much in
systems and work with abstract ideas, rather than existentially. Our
group was essentially a lay group in its thinking.

Q. What kind of discoveries did people make?

A. The young woman studying sociology was living with her
husband under strain in a precarious and dangerous situation. The
couple were helping to organize peasants and industrial workers to
stand up for their rights. She came to the workshop asking herself
whether she should leave her husband or not. Because I understood part of her situation, I asked her to study the material from
the Sermon on the Mount on anxiety – seek first the kingdom of
God and his righteousness and all other things shall be added.

As she began to grapple with this portion of the biblical message and to work out the first outline of the material she would write, she came to me trembling and in tears, saying 'I am the Christian of the two. My husband is an atheist. And yet I am the one who has given in to anxiety. I did not understand what it means to live by faith as I seek for social justice in Peru.' She became really transformed as she realized that God *expected* her to live without care for material things, and that this was part and parcel of the posture that she and her husband had already taken in their search and struggle for social justice. Her fresh understanding of this biblical passage opened a door to the whole area of the promise of God, to a new world which is both here and to come. She saw that this new world is here and now, to the extent to which she lives through the power of Christ. It is also on its way, and this will give her hope and faith that hers is not a frustrating and a lost struggle.

I think one of the most dramatic group experiences – I believe firmly in the interaction of group dynamics in this whole process – was an attempt to capture the essence of the whole Sermon on the Mount and put it into one lesson. The person I asked to take responsibility for this, although coming from a very limited conservative evangelical background, was very well equipped. As she studied the Sermon on the Mount and kept looking in her concordance for related passages she came upon such questions as 'Lord, Lord, I have done all these things; will you let me into your kingdom?', to which the Lord says, 'I don't know you, I have never seen you before, go away'.

These passages spoke to her in a new way. Finally, she became very excited. She began to think of situations in which she had condemned others, where she had not loved her enemies, and these brought a real sense of penitence. I thought the time had come for the total group to share with her in order to begin to understand this. We began a brain-storming session. For example, the rich young ruler comes and says, 'Lord, I have obeyed all the commandments', but Jesus says to him, 'But it won't be that way among you; it is more than that'. I suggested to the group that we continue this line of thinking: 'Well I have done this and that; but Jesus says no – there's more to it.' As we explored all this in relation to contemporary behaviour, a new richness developed. 'I don't drink, I don't smoke, I don't dance, Lord; may I come into your kingdom?' and the Lord says, 'No, I am sorry, it's more than that.'

Then we said, 'All right Lord, what is it?' Once again, we entered into a group process of searching for what is the 'more'.

The group began to express itself almost in a form of a litany.

After we had gone through the whole exercise, which took perhaps two hours, I asked each member of the group to try to capture the insight in the form of a poem, or a litany, because we could see that it had a refrain: 'No, among you it will not be this way, it is more. Lord, what is it? It is this.' One person came up with a telling bit of poetry which will form the basis of our material on the subject. We began to see how the parables, those of the light and the mustard seed, for example, became symbols of this new thing which was being created as people began to learn and to live in the redeemed community. We made a new parable. Someone referred to the idea of Jesus giving water that will not cause thirst but will leap forth into eternal life. This idea of water lead someone else to say, 'Well, it is like an oasis in a desert. Wherever there is a spring, life breaks out. It can be just a small place – here, there, somewhere else. The kingdom is like this. There are signs of community here and there, even in the midst of the desert. But when the final day comes and the fullness of the kingdom arrives, as it will, the whole desert will be green.'

To me all this is imaginative theological thinking. I believe profoundly that the church's theological thinking has to be related to people's life situations or else it has no meaning. Lay people think dramatically, in pictures and experiences. They have a natural gift for doing theology.

Q. Did a fresh understanding of the Christian hope dominate the discussions?

A. I would say so. For example, two of the teachers told me at the beginning of the workshop that they knew nothing about theology. They were ready to turn around and go home. One of them was assigned to work on the anticipation people had as John the Baptist began to preach. As she worked with the biblical material, she was stimulated by the realization that there was an expectation which governed the life of people then which was intended to govern our life now. They and we are to wait and hope for some real evidence of God's presence among us. She was able specifically to relate the material to the contemporary experience of a community where she had been working. It was in North Chile. A drought had occurred which went on and on. The fields dried up. The cattle began to die. Week after week passed and no relief was in sight. They waited, feeling helpless, unable to do any work, unable to provide enough food to save the cattle. Then they came to themselves. 'Here we are', they said, 'calling ourselves Christians and yet beaten by circumstances. How should we act to show that we hope in God?' They talked it through and came to two main decisions. Instead of letting cattle die off haphazardly, they distributed the food so that breeding pairs were preserved. They could not plant crops, so they built a much-needed road. So when the rains came they were able to build up the herd again, and farm more efficiently because they had the extra asset of the road. This became for us a parable of our whole life.

The other teacher was asked to write on how the Holy Spirit gives us the power to share in the creation of the new world. The Holy Spirit had been a name without meaning for her. Yet as she studied the resurrection and ascension stories and the Pentecost passages she began to reflect upon other experiences she had in her life that she hadn't been able to explain. Promptings which she had felt and which she had followed had resulted in amazing things happening both in her family and in her life as a teacher. She came to realize that whenever she obeyed these leadings she found blessing, and began to understand that probably there had been others which she had disobeyed and therefore had got herself into situations that didn't bring blessing. The whole concept of the Holy Spirit as a power to life and creative effort came alive for her.

Q. Did it all end on a high note, or quietly?

A. I must fill in a bit more of the background to answer that question. The place we chose for the workshop was a Roman Catholic retreat house, run by nuns. From the start they took a keen interest, seeking to understand what we were doing, looking for an opportunity to talk to us. Then to our surprise, one day they asked us if we would like to participate with them in their mass. This threw our group into quite a turmoil. Some members had lived through quite severe persecution at the hands of Roman Catholics. We had to face the question of what it means to live in the new world Christ is building – communion together at one table?! We had a very frank and lively conversation. The Lutheran pastor said that he had had to have written permission from his church even to be present in this house; he felt he could not share in a eucharist without explicit permission. Nevertheless he agreed that we should go ahead. So we celebrated the mass. We taught one another our songs and these were used in the service. It was a new experience for some of us to receive communion with a priest presiding. Not all of our group took communion, though all of them participated in spirit.

The last session was planned to take the form of a Messianic Celebration. We began working on something which could be developed in the local church. But then it became clear to us that we must celebrate together with the nuns. We approached them, and they were very eager to take part. We agreed to prepare a common meal, an *agape*; and we worked out the litany and the form of service (which will be appearing in Book 9 of our New Life in Christ Course).

All this we did together with the nuns, some of whom confessed that they had never even spoken with an 'evangelical' before. Some of our group were equally surprised to find themselves participating in worship with Catholics – since this had been an impossibility in the past, and they had thought it would continue to be an impossibility in the future. We chose a woman deacon to preside, because she was at that point the only acting pastor among us. This was also symbolic for us.

Sunday dawned, a beautiful day, and our work was done. This was the first time that a book had ever been completed in such an amazing fashion, and we went outside just to sing. We had decided not to have a worship service. But something took hold of the group. Spontaneously we began to give expression to our sense of having lived during the last two or three days in a real eschatological community and to our sense that what we had been writing about had become a lived experience – not only for the group, but for the total community, including the nuns. You would almost have to describe what then developed as a 'conversion experience'. People who for many years had called themselves Christians suddenly took on a new radiance; they understood so many things in a different perspective, and gave witness to this spontaneously. Throughout the day we lived a kind of joy and exaltation which we could not attribute to anything else but the gift of the Spirit. When the Celebration took place, almost everyone (some of the nuns did not partake of the elements but they were certainly doing so in spirit) accepted it as a new experience of the grace of God, because we could not call it anything else. In this living way, we can say that as we understood and then wrote out the message we *experienced its validity*. We had participated in a sign that the new world had really come among us.

### Primary Theology

The kind of exercise which engages lay people in theological thinking, writing and other forms of expression must be accompanied by and stem from the recognition that crucial work of theology is done almost unnoticed, by people in their daily lives. Those who are trained in theology need to develop a new kind of hearing-on-the-spot to appreciate the character and quality of the theological work being done in this way.[16] The natural instinct of the professional is always to secure his own base, treat new thought as raw material to handle on his own terms, and draw new enterprises on to the territory with which he is familiar. That kills its quality.

'Contextual theology' is a promising emphasis made by many professional theologians. It insists that the theological weight of any fact or event can only be appreciated if the situation and surrounding circumstances of each such fact or event, and the attitudes and backgrounds of those involved, are taken fully into account. But what this may result in is a substantial adjustment of perspective, not a fundamental change. Can you take a tree, struggling for its life in an over-populated forest and examine it in a laboratory to understand the meaning of its struggle – even if you remove it with all the earth about its roots? Theological laboratories are, in such instances, still not being put under challenge as appropriate workplaces for the making of theology. A concern for contextual theology which thrusts people into pressured situations to gain their insights there, is quite a different matter.

What has been called 'waterbuffalo theology', comes even nearer to the mark. The phrase was coined to feature the assertion of Professor Kosuke Koyama of Singapore that whatever gifts and training he had had relevance only if they were put at the service of the humblest rice farmer, working with his waterbuffalo.[17] If what was said made no sense to such a man in his life, then it made no sense. So the gauge of theological illumination was not one's fellow scholars, or ecclesiastical leaders, but the poor man going about his life. This is a great advance, an attempt to find a true touchstone. Yet, in the end, it leaves the initiative where it was. It is those who have had professional training in theology who are responsible for seeing to it that there is this kind of relevance in theological work. They still 'bring the gospel of Christ' to others.

But the tables need to be turned. The whole church must be reinherited as the theological community. The theological laboratory must become a support agency, and not remain the unquestioned initiating agency.

Professional theologians can be perceptive interpreters – *if they leave where they are* and live in touch with the sources. Primary theology is theology hammered out by the people of God themselves on the anvil of their fire and suffering. It provides the 'resources centre' for all other theological work.

Once this is recognized it may be possible to give confidence to those who are equipped theologically to use their equipment discriminatingly and decisively, in ways which are at present being neglected.

Once it is acknowledged that the main work of the professional theologian is auxiliary to the total theological task; once it is acknowledged that the theological community is the people of God and not just specialists; once it is acknowledged that primary theology represents a vast, little-explored oilfield of theological resources: justice may at last be done to features of theological work which are being obscured in our day. There are more distinctive services to be rendered and more distinctive initiatives to be taken by the professional than have yet been mentioned.

We are in a time when, thanks to the mass media, there is a developing awareness of how others in the world are placed and of the need for this to be one world. It is a time when guilt settles like dust on middle-class people who know themselves to be privileged. They want to stop thinking and get involved. They want to get alongside the deprived. To some extent this may be selfish, a move to get rid of guilt feelings. But it may also be healthy. They should then ask what gifts they are to bring, to set alongside those of the gifted underprivileged. It may be that the very things they have begun to despise – capacity for analysis and articulation, experience of 'the system' and how to work or combat it, ranges of knowledge which are outside the compass of the disinherited – are the gifts which begin to take on relevance, once they are engaged where it matters. It is a pity when the owner of a timber yard, converted by his engineer son to a new view of the world, throws all his wood into the river and goes with him to live among the poor – only to find that what the poor most need is a bridge across that very river to a market on the other side.

There are times when professionals must take a situation by the scruff of the neck and give determined leadership (as campfollowers are said to have done at a crucial moment in the battle of Bannockburn). If primary theology runs to seed, and develops unchecked populist tendencies, then nothing is more needed to restore its true face than good scholarship, and the gifts of psychological understanding and sociological and historical perspective which that can provide to clarify revelation. The rise of Mariolatry over the centuries cried out for just such disciplined treatment. Theologians let the church down where they did not use the critical tools which were properly theirs. Trained theologians who connive at the uncritical development of devotion simply because it may offer immediate advantage to the church are not 'listening to the poor' but simply failing in the responsibilities required by their proper discipline.

## 3  An End to Missions and Mission Fields

Today, the quality and character of the flow of Christian missions from the Atlantic region to the rest of the world are being brought under question by those who also acknowledge the life-giving things they brought. Does this give hope that we might be brought up sharp – that we might come to ourselves, that our relations to 'developing' countries might undergo serious change?

The danger is a lively one that people who have put money and prayer into overseas mission, if they were exposed to some of its worst effects, would get disenchanted. But we must seriously ask if this ought not to be risked. In reality missions overseas have been such a mixed success. We have too long avoided the fact that, in questions of world mission, the truth is at stake. Is a withdrawal of support which may go with a serious rethinking of mission in the world we live in, with account taken of the total picture, not to be undertaken for the sake of the truth? How can 'home churches' be re-educated for mission in their own place without facing the facts?

A second danger lies in this. In many parts of the world, those who have suffered from the harshest effects of mission have found a voice. Through the mass media that voice has been heard. A breed of less docile missionaries has confirmed the testimony. Reaction could now go to two extremes. Some might feel that the missionary enterprise must simply be written off. Others might hold that it has been under fierce fire for quite long enough, and that criticism must stop.

Those who are harsh in their criticisms may not take enough account of the fact that everything the church does is historically conditioned. No church can live in detachment from the stream of history in which it is set. This stream is one of the things which helps to shape its identity and task at any particular point in history. What is required of the church is not that it should try to stand outside that stream, but that it should stand critically within it. The fault of the church in mission has been its inadequate self-criticism as it had undertaken its work.

As we look back from the perspective of the present time, we can see glaring faults. But we who look are also conditioned by our history. Almost certainly we are, in different ways, every bit as insensitive and callous. We have a right to make judgments on the past only if we take its lesson to heart – by examining the ways in which we may be betraying the gospel in our time. We are under judgment, and will one day be appalled at our own crassnesses.

But should this silence us? Has there been quite enough 'knock-ing of missions'?

In some quarters, there has been intensive research, self-question-ing and debate. But how much of this has got out into the churches? How much of it has reached the ears of ordinary Christians? How seriously is the damage done by missions appreciated and seen in proportion to the blessings?

On the whole, Christian people committed to mission overseas have had as yet almost no chance to feel on their pulses what it has been like to be at the 'other end' of the outreach which extended from their own northern climes to other parts of the world. We have no chance of coming to our senses as the People of God unless the impact of that experience and criticism is taken.

What will be hard to bear is the revelation that our cultures which have, for centuries, presented themselves as personifications of 'civilization' are in so many respects barbarous and immature. What will be hard to bear is the revelation of the loathing poorer peoples feel for those who have acted towards them seemingly with the best of intentions. What may be hardest to bear is that missions are so often classified as simply an expression of white domination, uncritically part of that domination. The very word 'mission-field', which defines some people in terms of others' self-giving and en-thusiasm, is anathema. Land ownership, denomination, race, medical and educational work can all be vehicles of patronage.

The policy of missionary agencies which moved into South Africa included the securing of areas of land. On this, churches, schools, technical training enterprises were built – and the benefit of these to the people of that area is fully acknowledged. Land was also wanted for cultivation. It was rented to selected families. But there were two serious impediments. (*a*) Every attempt on the part of Africans to *buy* land for themselves was resisted. (*b*) You had to be a Christian of the right colour to get your education.[18] So an insistence on dependency and the promotion of a denomination were laid down as terms for coming within the hearing of the gospel.

The religious dependence of Africans opened the door wider to their political treatment as children, who cannot be expected to know their own minds and need others to make decisions for them. The desire for denominational security and status produced a strong tendency towards conformity with the policies of powers-that-be.

A black South African pastor, taking a course of studies in Britain, was asked what he felt was the main legacy of the mis-sionary movement in South Africa. With deep feeling, he replied, 'Racialism. Christ has been blasphemed.'

Why must the churches press home the World Council of

Churches' Programme to Combat Racism – or find an alternative, more radical and effective programme, if they cannot accept that one? Why must the churches put pressure on governments, commercial enterprises and banks to stop the profitable investment in Southern Africa which feeds on the low-paid labour of whole peoples who live in unfreedom? Because Christian missions helped to establish and consolidate the disease of racialism. At points of history at which a road might have been hewn out to adjust and equalize society, the churches through their missions, allowed racist policies to operate and be perpetuated. They did not stand up for Africans as for people made in the image of God. So churches are not being invited to do any greatly courageous or daring thing when they are asked to use the undoubted power they have to effect a change of mentality in the Western world and press for alternative policies regarding the wealth gained from investment in Southern Africa. They are simply being asked to notice the sewers left by their past and to take account of the millions who have been left sick and diseased by their existence.

The provision from the West of hospitals, schools, training institutions may be thought of as inevitably beneficial to local populations in Africa, Asia, Latin America and Oceania. But Orthodox communities interpret much of this provision as bribes to win converts. You will not be long in Egypt and in touch with the Coptic Orthodox Church before you become aware of their understanding of the dynamic of missions from the West in the last two centuries. Missionaries came bent on converting Moslems. They found them too tough. So, to justify their existence, they changed course and, on the basis that their Orthodox brethren needed renewal, proselytized, detaching many from their own communities of faith. Hospitals, schools etc. provided useful bait to catch souls.

Once they gain independence, many countries cannot afford to sustain the expensive buildings and equipment of Western hospitals. They need medical care which is simpler, less costly and most widely distributed among the people. Others see, in these institutions, inbuilt assumptions about values and ways of life which are a noose around their necks when they struggle to assert their own identity and the values of their own culture.

Now that the assumptions underlying educational systems are being widely questioned, there is a fresh awareness of the extent to which the educational work of missions from traditional sending areas has been directed to the equipping of élites who, through education, are enabled to retain leadership positions in a country and deny them to the humbler members of communities. Missionary education has performed a definite political function, strengthening traditional power groups at the expense of the rest of the community.

Over their heads, the Gurindjis, an Aboriginal tribe in Australia, had their tribal lands taken away. They were leased by the government to a British-based company, who developed a big cattle station. The Aboriginals became stockmen and cattle hands. Their pay was subsistence provision – little more than flour, sugar and tea. They no longer owned their own life. It was lived on terms which others imposed. No voice of Christian protest was raised.

In 1966 they quietly walked off the land *en masse*.

They could not be lured back by the offer of better wages. For they had lost things much more precious than money. Their need was nothing less than to regain identity with themselves and with the sacred land.

What they basically rejected was foreign ownership of land which they knew to be theirs. What they sought was what still lived in their bones: the knitting up of their own world with that of their ancestors; the restoration of the old community form of organization which allowed them to live with dignity as brothers and sisters, sharing possessions; the burial of the boss/worker division between human beings. Their Moses was Vincent Lingari.[19] Their wilderness was a dry river bed. Manna was food brought by students and voluntary associations to sustain their life when it looked as if they must starve. Their Promised Land was Wadi Creek where, again with quiet assurance, moving out in due time from the river bed, they fenced in part of their own land and began there to build their houses, rear their cattle and develop their own style of communal life. They made no secret of their intention – to take back their land a bit at a time. The quiet authority of their act, as they went about it without a weapon in their hands, in the end overcame opposition. The Labour Government in Australia took back the leased land from the British Company and secured it for them. But white-claimed Australian land never passes easily to the meek. It has to be reclaimed by the meek using the power of their powerlessness.

When people are deprived of their own land, denied their traditional life-in-community, broken off from the precious living relationship with the dead, given no alternative but to work for a pittance – and no Christian voice is raised, how can Christianity be understood as other than an accomplice in enslaving transactions?

The need for religious faith often goes deep with those who turn their backs on a way of life which has let them down. From Six Nations in Grand River Lands in Canada, an Iroquois points out: 'Marx and Engels drew from the social structure of the Iroquois to build their social dreams upon (Frederick Engels, *The Origin of the Family, Private Property and the State*). And the US patterned their government after the Iroquois government. But then both left out the most important thing – the religion upon which both the government and social system is based.' Again he writes: 'Most Indians ... are still concentrating on legal, racial and social issues – to ensure that they get security, respect and recognition from other men. They mostly have lost their religions and cannot apparently see that their security and recognition should come from the Creator. We here at Six Nations are lucky enough to have our religion – through 300 years of various pressures, military, cultural, economic, racial, etc., our religion (which is the base of our culture) has kept us together and free from extinction.' Accordingly, in what seems to be a forlorn 'back to the land' move (first in the reserve and then, once experience is gained, in the wilderness) his family and a few other families are going out like the Gurindjis but without their experience: 'There are some of us here at Six Nations who are willing to try to rebuild our tattered culture and exist independent from the spiritually dead White Society'. They acknowledge: 'We are all amateurs at the task of rebuilding a nation and a culture. The Jews are also trying to do something like this, I suppose. We have some problems in common with them, for example – what is a Jew? What is an Indian? – and neither definition can be made without reference to religion.' Dignity, community, roots – these again seem to be basic elements in the search: 'We would begin taking in our "grandmothers" and "grandfathers" as soon as we began to function. Perhaps the unwanted children also.'

They are turning their backs on the white man's ways and the white man's God who has not stretched out a hand to help – and going back to the Long House religion of their ancestors.

What else is there to do if Christianity has proved to be simply part of an oppressive system?

Another Amerindian has written in anger: 'To us, Hitler killing 6 million was not the world-shaking event it was to Europe – from our vantage point of having over 20 million killed by Europeans, of having whole nations of Indians completely destroyed.' He goes on: 'Who is oppressing Indians in general? Only the US, Canada, Brazil, Mexico, Peru and the other "governments" of those two continents? Who is oppressing, then, the natives of Australia and of Africa? Who benefits from the rubber, chocolate, petroleum, minerals and timber of North and South America? Western civilization *as a whole* – Europeans (who may enjoy calling themselves Americans, Australians or whatever). And I almost insist that there is no Christianity *except that which exists*. That spoken of and thought of by theologians cannot really concern us who must fight the effects of what exists in the real world.' And again: 'Can you look at the world and say that western civilization is good? Can you look at the world and say that Christianity, as it is, is good?'

We are hearing more, these days, about rubbed out Indian peoples who were supposed to have been consigned safely to oblivion. IDAC document 4 on 'Political Education – An Experience in Peru' may be allowed to make some of its main points through extracts, about the Aymara Indians:

Destruction of the Aymara socio-economic life was accompanied by the imposition, at the hands of the Catholic clergy, of an authoritarian and oppressive deity completely foreign to Aymara cosmology. (page 3)

To fit in and be productive in a capitalist society, the Aymara had to change their whole value system and world vision. (page 5)

Resignation and acceptance of suffering – so fervently preached by the priests – had become prevailing attitudes. (page 17)

They drew up a list of people who had exploited all these groups. Included were landlords, owners of mines, government bureaucrats, priests (with a few exceptions), military men and police. (page 18)

In Ilesha in Nigeria, a group from the local community met under the chairmanship of the Ven. U. E. I. Felope to contribute to the 'Participation in Change' programme. One of the questions used to focus discussion was 'what should be prominently on the agenda of the 1975 Fifth World Assembly of the WCC?'. The chairman summed up contributions from the floor and made his own emphasis in the following words: 'Christianity came through the West to us. But Westerners are not acting at all like Christians towards us. The inhumanity, exploitation and oppression which we suffer, coming from those from whom Christianity originally came, hurts us and shames the church. I went to an Anglican church when I was in Geneva a short time ago, and it was so obvious that people were unwilling to sit beside me – the church of the West is full of racialism. The churches of the West have the money and the power – but they need to learn from the rest of the world what real humanity means.

'Evangelism to the West is badly needed. A rebirth of genuine Christianity needs to be produced. The gospel is being brought into disrepute by the people who had originally been its bearers and representatives. The big question for the Fifth Assembly is how can the World Council of Churches begin a mission to the West to evangelize people there in all their dealings with other countries? There is nothing more important than this to face.'

A dominating flow of history, based on wealth and technology, has been as much a mark of missions from the West as it has been of the theology of the West. People have been crushed and silenced by the gospel which makes free. They turn from it, sick in the stomach, to search for true life elsewhere. If they care at all about the faith, they have no doubt about where the main field of mission lies – on our doorsteps.

*Reappraisal*

'But ... but ... but ...' may come the protests in their turn, 'Who preached the gospel to you? Who set up hospitals and schools and churches? Who brought you into the stream of world civilization? What do you really hold against us?'

There are many kinds of arrogance.

Usually arrogance is thought of as a personal attribute. Christian missionaries have not been exempt from charges of *personal* arrogance. But humility and dedication have been more frequent hallmarks. That does not, however, exclude other forms of the same sin. *Cultural* arrogance is one. It may be expressed in the assumption that, as the bearer of one's own culture, one is the bearer of true and definitive ways of living. The history of Christian mission is very mixed here – some missionaries really entered into the whole context of the societies to which they came, so that there was a healthy interflow of cultural influences, while others acted as if their way of life were unquestionably superior and should simply replace indigenous ways. The main point is not to work out how the record balances, but to help those in the traditional sending areas of the world to become vividly aware of what it feels like to be robbed of your culture by someone who is coming to do you good. There has been *institutional* arrogance – the setting up of forms and organizational means of church life which have simply been transplanted from outside (and which may be too technically difficult or expensive for locals to maintain by themselves). Only now is *educational* arrogance being recognized adequately; only now are people digging into their own traditional sources of knowledge and revaluing them. Personal, cultural, theological, organizational, educational gifts have been brought to societies in the Third World – that is not to be denied. What has to be seen in the same perspective is the arrogance which marked much of the bringing.

There are also different *styles* of arrogance. From two in particular the 'receiving' countries feel they have suffered. The more obvious one is positive and aggressive. It results in people being made to feel that they are second-class citizens or worse. But the other form is equally destructive. Its hallmark is – being so wrapped up in one's own conviction of what is right and what is important that the effects of this on other people are not even calculated. One can be arrogantly self-enclosed in one's missionary vocation,[20] and thus be set over against the people one should be with. As Paulo

Freire has said, to end up without the people is another way of being against them,[21] however good one's intentions might be.

Whence comes the demand for the reassessment of the missionary enterprise so that it is seen in a more total context? Very substantially from Latin American, African and Asian Christians who have found place and voice in the ecumenical movement; who are now part of the stream of fresh self-assertiveness directed from colonized countries to ex-colonizers. These, the indigenous missionaries, have tried to point out the limited perspectives of earlier missions. But a great deal of the re-evaluation has also come from those who went themselves from the traditional 'sending' parts of the world to other parts. Things have been brought home to them which they realize need to be brought home to others. It is no gain to Christian mission if its enterprise is either romanticized or vilified. It simply must be looked at with open eyes. And eyes in the Northern Hemisphere can be opened only if ears are attentive to the experiences of indigenous peoples.

A reserve in Zululand in South Africa was built by people who were unfortunate enough to live in what became designated as a white zone. One day they had their homes bulldozed, and their bits of furniture put on lorries. They were taken out into the open veldt where, without water, electricity, roads, sewerage or any such thing they had to start a new life from scratch. At one point a woman I was talking with mentioned the doings of teenage daughters. When I left her I said to my Zulu companions: 'I didn't quite catch her name. Mrs ...?' 'No, not Mrs, Miss ...' said my guide. Only later did I get the full story.

Before missionaries came to that area, the following custom obtained. If a mature young boy and girl fancied one another, with the consent of the parents he and she could summon their friends and they could discuss the possibility of sleeping together. If this were agreed, there were rules of the game. She would go to bed with him, but would have her legs tied. All kinds of sexual play would be allowed except penetration ('she had to remember her father's cattle' – a brideprice was involved in a marriage arrangement, and the whole extended family was implicated, so there must be no risk of a pregnancy from this experimental sexual contact.) Most often, this would be the only such casual encounter which would take place between the girl and someone she fancied. Most often she would marry someone else.

Into this society came white missionaries. They became aware of this practice and denounced it as a filthy one. If you were to become a Christian, you must abandon it.

They failed entirely to take account of the social basis on which the particular custom rested. In that society everyone was given a grounding in sex education from the earliest years. Imaginatively, instruction for the years when young people matured into adults was made the responsibility of older teenagers. By the time they came to marriage, young people were thoroughly knowledgeable.

The white missionaries paid no attention to this basis. They simply swept the custom away. No alternative sex aducation was provided. So Christian girls became known as 'easy game'. From that time to this, Christianity and illegitimacy have had a tie-up in that area.

Dr James Stewart, who became Principal of Lovedale in South Africa in 1870, founded the *Kaffir Express*.[22] In his second editorial, he wrote: 'Our aim is to scatter ideas in the moral wastes and desert places of heathen ignorance ...'

A contemporary publication reveals the persistence of such an attitude a hundred years later:

Native peoples suffer by contact with us. We over-awe them by certain superiorities, which they recognize immediately. We have no ground for boasting. These superiorities are products of the Gospel, products of what our Lord calls 'salt' working in our midst.... It is not our superior intelligence or brains which have procured for us what we have, but the Fountain of Morality from which we have drunk. What a native lacks is not brains but integrity, and this can come only from the Lord and Giver of life, through the Gospel.[23]

Haitians who were interviewed about the impact of missions on their own country, built up a picture which points to something like a state of missionary pollution. More than 160 missionary societies are at work in the country, and, of these, more than 80% have their personnel concentrated in Port au Prince, the capital.

How has this come about? What are the effects?

Haitians put the jig-saw together as follows:

We have an open-door policy.... We are within easy reach of the USA.... We can provide a strong selling line – we are 'riddled with poverty and superstition'. So people's sympathies can be touched.... It does not dawn on donors that the money that they are expending is all used up in their own expatriate personnel, and a few native ministers.[24] We are caught in a trap.

What do the Christian missionaries here look like? In the eyes of the people, they appear no different from invading rival salesmen, each asserting that his own brand is the only one which washes whiter than white. This is an obscuring of the Christian faith and a sheer hindrance to the development of the indigenous church....

Voodooism is strengthened. Because missionary agencies look like commercial firms trying to sell an imported product which really belongs elsewhere, voodooism by contrast comes to look like the religion of the land. The effect of missionary pressure is the opposite of what is intended.

Voodooism, which draws on deep African, Caribbean and Christian sources, heightens its appeal.[25]

The insensitiveness of missionaries has done a lot of damage to Haitian culture. Values and life-styles have been imported which just do not fit. A good selling line abroad, for instance, is the need for orphanages. There are plenty of orphans all right to fill them.

But the orphanages are run according to the life styles of the part of the world from which the finance comes. The children are brought up with alien values. They become deculturalized. The net effect is that once they come to adulthood, they turn out to be incapable of fitting into their own society.

Quite unintentionally, I suppose, missions have stripped us of the leadership we have badly needed. Our most promising people have been selected and sent abroad for training – to provide us with sociologists and development experts, for example. But this training is given against a background entirely different from our own. When these bright people return, they find they cannot adjust again to Haitian society; they have become strangers. So they move off to the culture with which they are now familiar, and the higher salaries which now attract them, i.e. to the USA. The result of the kind of training they have received is that they are lost to us. This drain of leadership has been produced by people who have shown concern but have worked from within their own terms of reference, not from within ours.

The work of the Centre Haitien d'Investigation de Sciences Sociales, an independent secular organization at the service of the ecumenical movement, which takes Haitian society and culture seriously, is a sign of hope. Instead of treating voodooism simply as an evil to be exorcized[26] or as a phenomenon to be studied objectively,[27] this group has tried to understand the function of voodoo in Haitian society. They have been able to say positive as well as negative things about it. For instance a good deal of the cultural shock that would await those who move from rural areas to the city, is alleviated by the bridge that voodooism throws to link life in the country with life in the town. The evil elements can be seen in their true light only if the positive contribution made to society is also given its due. Once important indigenous characteristics are valued people are freed to seek a fuller life beyond voodooism.

Thus the effects of overseas mission can be to splinter the human community, strip a country of its leadership, label the gospel as a foreign import and frustrate the growth of the indigenous church.

In North Western Kenya, the National Christian Council of Kenya came to the assistance of people affected by drought in what is largely a Muslim area. The situation was already much mitigated by the faithfulness with which those Muslims who had income set aside 10% for their needy brothers and sisters. The people were unwilling nomads, moving continually in the quest for adequate water supplies. The NCCK helped them to establish growth areas, on an inter-tribal basis, in the hope of producing change towards an economy based on agriculture.

One group, on receiving a bag of maize for sowing, dug a hole, buried the sack full of grain, and hoped for a harvest! Technical assistance was clearly needed. This was offered through missionary agencies. The missionaries who came saw the situation not only as a means for offering technical services but as an opportunity for proclaiming the gospel. Islam was looked upon as a realm of darkness from which Christ was absent. What the Muslim community needed was the deliverance that they, the missionaries, could offer. Now the African church in that area was in brotherly relationship with the Muslims. The attitude of the missionaries from abroad threatened to split the human community. It also menaced the reconciling potential of the growth areas. These had been cunningly located on the boundaries of different often hostile tribes, so that people at one and the same time would learn agricultural skills and learn to work together. So the local community made it quite clear that, while they were grateful for the technical help brought by the missionaries, they were not prepared to endure the kind of propaganda which accompanied it.

'A clear case where assistance from others who have different skills is acceptable, on the basis of a common humanity, but a deliberate programme of evangelization is not?' The question was put to a technical adviser who had lived with the tribes of that area for some months.

'No,' he replied, 'they are quite open to evangelization as well. But it must be evangelization by quality of life. By that they are prepared to be persuaded. "Evangelization" by word, carrying with it a wholesale and uninstructed condemnation of Islam and the things they have loved and cherished and respected, with all its consequences of divisiveness, is something they will not tolerate.'

The partitions of Japanese houses can be removed to provide a substantial meeting place in even quite small homes. One Sunday morning, some forty or fifty people gathered in such a home. Most of them were young adults. Some Western hymns were sung and some of Japanese origin. The readings were followed intently, and people really worked on the exposition of four different Bible passages although they did not discuss the interpretation aloud with the young pastor who was leading them. I did not need to know the language to be part of a vitalizing and refreshing experience.

'A pity about that,' said my guide as we left.

'A pity? Far from it! An exhilarating experience – even for a visitor from Europe!'

'I mean, it's rather a pity that this church grew as it did.'

'How did it grow then?'

'Well, one or two Christians moved into this area and discovered one another. They started to meet for Bible study and worship. Then the quality of their life started to attract others: most of the people you saw there came from Shintoism or some other faith, or no faith at all. It was the sheer quality of life of the original group which produced this church.'

'But that is all good – what worries you?'

'Well, you see, the original group was simply the church of this place, the Christians who happened to be here and who were drawn together by the common faith they were living out. But, unfortunately, they were all kinds: Roman Catholics, Baptists, Salvation Army, the lot.'

'But isn't that a good thing?'

'In one way. But then, we have not only heard the gospel from you Westerners, we have received your divisions. The people who have joined this house-church cannot be baptized. There is no one tradition into which they all may enter. The church cannot grow in its fullness.'

*Go! or stay ...*

It is in the light of experiences such as are related above that, at the hinge of the years 1972–1973, a conference of the Division of World Mission and Evangelism held in Bangkok turned serious attention to the possibility of a moratorium. One popular myth is that what was proposed was that there should be a complete halt to the transfer of missionary funds and personnel from one part of the world to another. What was really proposed was that, in places where people felt the oppression of the kind of strong influence from elsewhere which comes with funds and personnel, they should feel free to demand a breathing-space – and get this with the understanding of their brothers. What was wanted was room to allow those who have felt themselves under pressure by the wills and ways of life of others, to come out from under that pressure and discover their own identity. Money means power. Foreign personnel with money behind them (and some missionary societies will still not support projects requested by indigenous churches unless they send their own personnel both to vet them and to promote them) bring strong influences with them from the mentality and priorities of the sending agencies. What is being suggested is a very simple thing. If any church in any country, or any group of churches, feels it is not able to grow and thrive in a way which is rooted in the life and culture of that country without asking for the removal of pressures which keep preventing this natural growth, then it should be understood within the Christian fellowship that a temporary halt to outside aid has to be called. In some cases the moratorium will be on both money and people. In other cases the flow of personnel will be halted, but money will still be wanted. In the latter case, the attitude is not likely to be 'we depend on our richer brothers' but rather 'our brothers belong to a part of the world which has taken the riches of our countries to fatten its own standards of living – it is time to reclaim a small portion of what is ours by right'.

One of the most important recent statements on the future of mission originating in the traditional sending areas was made by Bishop F. Pagura to the Missionary Liaison Committee of Costa Rica, where he served until recently:

– If you cannot understand what is happening in this continent, in this hour in which it awakens to the dawn of a new liberation, Missionary, go home.

– If you are not able to separate the eternal word of the gospel from the cultural moulds in which you brought it to these lands and even taught it with true abnegation, Missionary, go home.

– If you cannot identify with the sufferings, anguish and aspirations of these peoples made prematurely old by an unequal struggle that would seem not to have end or hope, Missionary, go home.

– If your alliance and fidelity to the nation of your origin is stronger than your loyalty and obedience to Jesus Christ who has come to 'put down the mighty from their thrones and exalt those of low degree' (Luke 1.52), Missionary, go home.

– If your dogmatism is such that it does not permit you to revise your theology and ideology in the light of all the biblical testimony and the happenings of these times, Missionary, go home.

– If you are not able to love and respect as equals those whom one day you came to evangelize as 'lost', Missionary go home.

– If you cannot rejoice with the entrance of new peoples and churches into a new period of maturity, of independence, of responsibility, even at the price of committing errors such as those you and your countrymen committed also in the past, then it is time to return home.

– But if you are willing to share the risks and pains of this hour of birth which our American peoples are living, even denying yourself; if you begin to rejoice with them because of the joy of feeling that the gospel is not only announcement and affirmation of a remote hope, but of a hope and a liberation that is already transforming history; if you are willing to put more of your time, of your values, of your life at the service of these people who are awakening, then, stay, since there is much to be done, and hands and blood are needed for such an immense enterprise in which Christ is pioneer and protagonist.

## Hands and Blood are Needed

The fire of the Holy Spirit is running through the world. The mission of God is bringing missions under judgment. An inescapable feature of that judgment relates to damage done to peoples and their cultures by missions from the West. It would seem to be logical to bring such missions to an end.

But the situation is not so tidy.

Let us agree that the initiative in mission has come so overwhelmingly from one region of the world, that that region must now defer to initiatives developing elsewhere. Notwithstanding, the Spirit runs where it will. Even from the countries which, historically, have been the dominating ones, God will ask new things. Sometimes only someone moving into a situation from the outside can give the kiss of life. This impact from the outside is needed particularly in the West. But it will still be needed, at times, from the West.

Sister Victricia – a member of the ecumenical team working with ZOTO, the Tondo people's organization in Manila, the Philippines – made a point in 1972 which holds good. She was queried about the team's response to an invitation to offer certain support. Did this not inevitably mean accepting a position which would mean that the team would dominate the shanty town dwellers? Her reply was twofold. 1) If people feel helpless, outside help is nearly always necessary to provide the first spark. 2) One must be near enough the people to understand their aspirations and articulate them for them. Once the spark has taken hold, once people gain confidence to articulate their own aspirations, then the grace to withdraw and the timing of that withdrawal are all-important. From there, people must grow into their own responsibilities, in their own way and time.

In a quite different context, a similar point is made by Thomas Acton in a recent publication.[28] It concerns the politicizing of those supreme individualists, gipsies, through the intervention in their lives of non-gipsies. This seemed to him to be the only way to nurture gipsy nationalism. It illustrates the important role which may be played by middle-class people (the writer is a 'shy, self-confessed scholar') in relation to cultures which are quite foreign to them, the dangers of unprofitable interference, and the hard knocks which must be taken from 'a difficult, trying and seldom grateful minority group'. Acton notes the danger of arrogance; and goes on:

I know that gipsies have always had a sense of their own culture, but there haven't always been enough articulate, educated gipsies around to express it. I've seen my role really as someone helping the gipsies to deal with the Government. A sort of sociological gun-runner, getting them the weapons by showing them how to work on committees and how to operate the system.

Interference in other people's lives need not be for evil. For Christians it all stems from acknowledging a God who interferes in people's lives and in their history. One cannot escape: But one can act brashly or sensitively. It is a sign of the one community of Christian faith in its concern for the community of mankind that people flow across dividing lines to establish fellowship with one another and to offer service. There are two important factors which must be particularly held in mind by those who go overseas from Europe and North America. One is that we have done our own thing in our own way – and now we must gladly accept the position of being inserted into enterprises initiated and developed by 'the people of the land', their way.

The first of these factors may be illustrated as follows.

In a private interview given in February 1973, Pope Shenouda of the Coptic Orthodox Church said: 'When we give to one another in the world church, what have we a right to share? Theology and spirit, no more. If we also bring our culture, music, ways of life, methods of organizing and administering, language – that is imposition, a hindrance to the truth.' A difficult distinction to make – as is indicated by the ecclesiastical supervision exercised by his own church over the Ethiopian Orthodox Church up till the second half of this century! Yet his statement provides a fundamental insight and a warning against foisting on another people matters which belong to a missionary's own background and tradition. He or she may not be able to stand clear of a particular culture and way of life – but this means that he or she must be all the more aware of the fact, and give other cultures and other ways of life the fullest chance to provide their own environments for the gospel.

The second factor relates to the sure, fresh touch for mission being developed in many countries of the so-called Third World.

A significant style in mission is being expressed in a CELADEC[29] enterprise in Peru. A team of young people, all of them working-class in background and all of them educated, have chosen to live and work together in the midst of an impoverished community. They are using their teaching skills to help awaken the people to realize that they need not be victims of their miserable conditions but may change them. Thus they encourage them to make and implement decisions about their own future, at first in small ways, and then in greater ways, so that they begin to transform their whole situation and that of communal life around them. Ten of

them are engaged on the task but only four are in paid employment.[30]

The $72 per month earned by the four has to support the total
team and pay for teaching materials and apparatus as well. They
have put down their roots into the life of the people, accepted the
culture of the people, are learning the key words of the people
and using these to encourage the development of awareness and a
choice for freedom. They are educated, so they do not claim to
*be identified* with the community; but they are *identifying* with
them by the manner of their life.

They have crossed a financial frontier by adopting a simple style
of living which allows the income of a few to do for all. They
are taking the risk of faith – they have no certainty that the
$72 will continue to be available from one month to the next. They
have found an alternative to heavy financing from outside agencies.

They have crossed an educational frontier, giving up the opportunity to become cultural capitalists, returning and immersing
themselves among those who have little education or none.

They have crossed a class frontier, refusing the status available
to middle-class professionals, choosing rather to reinsert themselves
among those who are regarded as belonging to the lowest stratum
of society.

They have crossed a cultural frontier, deliberately deciding to
honour the culture of the lowly rather than the prestige culture for
which they could have opted.

They have crossed a frontier of individualism, for they act as
a team. At least three or four of them come to meet those to whom
they want to explain the work – so that it is clear that there is
shared leadership.

'Why do you do all this? What moves you?'

'We are Christians. That is what drives us.'

'Are you Catholics?'

'No, just Christians. We have no attachment to any religious
body.'

'Is your work here self-sufficient within your own country? Do
you need anything from other countries?'

'We all have need of one another in a world fellowship. Moreover, if the money we are receiving at present is withdrawn, it
may be impossible to continue our mission at all unless our basic
daily needs can be met from elsewhere. We would also be helped
by having some more equipment.'

They walk on water.

Action Apostoloque takes seriously the growing conviction in
the world church about the value of missionary teams made up
of members from different cultures and countries. Its work in

Dahoméy represents a new attempt on the part of French-speaking churches and agencies to work together in mission, and to be genuinely at the service of the local community in each place in which they operate. Thus in the Fon area of Dahoméy there is a team from different countries and churches which accommodates itself to the style of life of the local people who are, in the main, animists.

Since there are many villages to contact, identification with rural people cannot be as complete as it was in the Peru example. But the approach shows solidarity with the villagers from the start.

Five people make up a team. Two nurses work round the clock from the moment of their arrival in a village, for there is much illness to cope with. The pastor goes out alongside the farmers and works with them in the fields. The youth worker gathers the young people, and, with their agreement and co-operation, starts clearing some spare ground for a games field. The 'basic educator' (*educateur de base*) works either in the fields or with the young people. A common factor is the manual work alongside the villagers. Another factor which binds people naturally together is the aware-ness of the presence of God – which one finds so vivid in so many parts of Africa. In the evenings they talk together about life, with the Bible as a reference source. After a week the team leaves, having stirred up all kinds of ideas and opened opportunities for a better life. In a month or two they will be back: to work, to discuss farm-ing and faith, and to worship with the people.

'Are you not still an invading force, manipulating poor villagers into unfamiliar patterns of life?'

'The gospel brings with it the compulsion to reshape life. But you are right to ask us to be alert. For it is not *we* who are to reshape it but Christ and the people together. We find it necessary, for example, to discard our usual Sunday liturgy for those who are taking their first steps in worship. A firm liturgy would impose a framework and constrict them. Rather, we let everything develop spontaneously. People make up their prayers out of their own griefs and joys. They sing songs developed from their own folk-lore tradition, songs from the fields. We try to help them to take the measure of Christian faith in their own way and in their chosen time so that they can retain the gifts of their culture and the insights into life-in-community which they held as animists, if they become Christians.'

An enterprise in Uganda came from two sides – indigenous initiative and resources provided from abroad (particularly skills for the development of group consultation and action). A report of what happened in one area can speak:

The pastor opened with prayer. A member of the team led a short bible study that spoke about the gifts that God had given his people to use in his service. Then the purpose of the gathering was explained and the way of working. When everybody was happy to proceed it was suggested that the group discuss and list the main problems people faced in the area.

This was a good starter for the group. It helped people to produce, themselves, the material with which they were to work. The local group must take responsibility for deciding what they want to work on, what they think is important, because they are going to be responsible for acting on whatever may emerge. The Kiru group actually produced 15 main problems. Because they were in fact one group, the men were encouraged to expand the items they had listed. (Ideally, with two or more small groups, they report to each other and compare lists.)

When the group had talked over the report it was possible to move on to the second task. Which of these problems did they think was the most important? Why was it a problem? What causes it? The group now had to *select*, to narrow down to one particular thing on which to work. The Kiru group decided that *poverty* was the most serious problem people faced. They saw it as a church problem in that people were either unable or unwilling to support the church properly. But it was also seen clearly as a community problem. In their report they showed poverty entered into most of the other problems. There was laziness and drunkenness – but they recognized there was also discouragement at much labour for little reward, with unreliable rains and other hazards of the climate. When they examined this problem they found its root in *ignorance*. People would be less poor if they used their land better. In one sense they were far from poor as they had many cows, but this form of wealth was not properly used. People would be better off if there was more cooperation in the community.

And so the third question. What do you think you might do to overcome this problem? An invitation to think of as many things as possible. 16 suggestions were made, some vague, but others very practical. They pointed particularly to the importance of education through the home, getting more help from trained people provided by government, getting people to cooperate more on the land as in the past, helping people to budget, persuading people not to keep so many cows. Finally they decided to call a meeting for all the community, to explain and talk over what they had discovered.

Here were 15 men at the centre who belong to their community but who know themselves and are known by others as Christians. They did not begin by discussing mission, the task of the church. But as they reflected on their community and pinpointed its problems, they came alive. They committed themselves to *do* something for the others, as part of the Christian church, making itself a *servant* for the sake of the whole community. What is being sensed of genuine concern is probably more important than any direct message in word about the faith.

I talked with a small group of Africans who had taken part in one of these ventures. They had been appointed by a village complex embracing about 700 people to take part in a preliminary survey of the situation of their community. After the process described, they went back to their people, reported on the issues that they had considered to be most important, and invited them to consult together about these. On the date in question, more than 500 of the 700 participated, dividing into groups to consider each of the issues, reporting back, then working out their priorities as a total community. 'But was this whole thing not an imported operation from Europe which you simply accepted and fitted in with?' I asked the group. Their spokesman replied, 'Rather we felt we were recovering something which belonged to us. In my grandfather's grandfather's time if there were some great matter which concerned the good and the future of the whole village, the Chief would assemble us and tell us what we had to face together. We would then discuss it for as long as was needed – for the whole of that day, and the next if need be, and the next if required, until we came to a common mind. Women had exactly the same freedom to contribute as men. When we had decided what we were going to do together, we worked out a part that each of us would take to achieve what was decided, and then went off to make the needed changes. What happened in our village area was the nearest thing to our own traditional way of life that we have seen for generations.'

The hard-won experience of the Third World is the chief resource of the traditional sending areas as they learn to appreciate the arrogance implied in 'missions' and 'mission fields', and seek with fresh eagerness participation with all peoples in the mission of God.

## NOTES

1. Nan Partridge, *Not Alone*, SCM Press 1972.

2. Karl Jaspers identifies the present time as the second axial period in human history (the first being the 8th Centry BC) – a period in which history takes a decisive turn so that it can never be the same again.

3. Every human being – including exalted human beings – is due respect. Respect and deference are entirely different things.

4. Those who read this book will at least not be economically poor.

5. As happened.

6. The one quoted took place on 13–25 November 1972.

7. To be accurate, ZOTTO in its earliest stage. Now Zone One Tondo Organization.

8. Imaginatively the Church of Scotland appointed a technological adviser some years ago, and were ready to play a responsible part in the oil boom – See 'Scotland in Turmoil', *Home Board of the Church of Scotland*, 1973.

9. One outstanding example is the International Documentary Service, IDOC, which, without fear or favour, exposes some of the raw sores and hopeful growth points of man's life in the world and in the church. Its 'Future of the Missionary Enterprise' documentation is particularly relevant.

10. My italics.

11. From the texts of the speeches as they were delivered.

12. Although indebtedness to them is freely acknowledged.

13. In old Scots the word 'maker' or 'makar' indicates the creative person, the person of insight. He or she would not be a systematizer, but a poet who saw deeply into the life of the common people, of whom he or she was one.

14. i.e. sleep on the floor there, not in a nearby hotel.

15. A clear role of the professional theologian is to set all this in the communion of saints, so that it is nourished and corrected by the hard-won experience of the church throughout history.

16. As one of the earliest worker-pastors, I went straight from theological college in 1942 to work as a labourer in industry. After a year or so, a local minister asked me what the men talked about during the ten-minute 'smoke-times'. 'Women they are chasing, dogs they race on the track, their wages, their kids, their gardens ...' I replied. 'I don't mean that' said the pastor, 'I was wondering if they ever have spiritual conversation at such times'. 'Oh yes, they do: they speak of the women they are chasing, the dogs they are racing, wages, kids, gardens ...'
If you cannot hear what people believe and where they stand when they speak in these terms, you will never hear at all.

17. 'On my way to the country church, I never fail to see a herd of water-buffalos grazing in the muddy paddy field. This sight is an inspiring moment for me. Why? Because it reminds me that the people to whom I am to bring the gospel of Christ spend most of their time with these water-buffalos in the rice field. The waterbuffalos tell me that I must preach to these farmers in the simplest sentence structure and thought development. They remind me to discard all abstract ideas and to use exclusively objects that are immediately tangible.' Kosuke Koyama, *Waterbuffalo Theology*, SCM Press 1974 p. vii.

18. An African participant in a USPG Conference in High Leigh, Hoddesdon, Hertfordshire, in January 1974, said he had had to get baptized three times to get where he was. One denomination required his baptism as a child if he were to get the benefit of its schooling. A second denomination required his baptism as an adult before they would permit him to get married. A third denomination provided grants which enabled him to do further studies, provided he was one of them – a status which had to be sealed by a third rite.

19. One of those men who have a way of going about life which makes the words 'human dignity' quite inadequate. Such people do not need to 'act with dignity' – they have such an assured touch for what belongs to the essentials of life that that assurance is enough. This is exactly what makes the Kimbanguist Church so impressively different in world ecumenical gatherings. It shows up the older churches to be, not so much pretentious as immature, by comparison.

20. And so be 'a seed which remains solitary', John 12.24.

21. *Pedagogy of the Oppressed*, Herder and Herder, p. 23.

22. Now the *South African Outlook*.

23. From the Introduction: D. Vaughan Rees, *'The Jesus Family' in Communist China*, Paternoster Press 1964.

24. Conversion to a new denomination is almost irresistible for a poor pastor who knows that if he goes over with all his flock his salary will be on an altogether different scale.

25. Several of the primitive painters who designed the remarkable biblical murals of the Episcopal Church in Port au Prince later went back to voodooism.

26. Frequently the 'missions' approach.

27. By and large the UNESCO approach. Secular agencies are equally criticized for working within terms of reference with which they are familiar, and which they import, rather than the terms of reference appropriate to the country.

28. Thomas Acton, *Gipsy Politics and Social Change*, Routledge & Kegan Paul 1974.

29. Latin American Evangelical Commission for Christian Education.

30. Noted in the winter of 1972/1973. The position is likely to be very little changed.

# II

## *Our God, 'A Consuming Fire'*

To live with and listen to groups of marginalized people who come from all Christian traditions and none, as they claim their dignity and place, and assert a right to participate in shaping their own future is to be pushed back to the Bible with new insights and new questions.

### 4  *The Place of the Poor*

Poverty, as one comes across it in the world, would seem to have as a fundamental characteristic the loss of what it takes to make life really human.

There are people who have been rubbed out, who draw a mask of inscrutibility over the rape of their manhood or womanhood, aware they count for nothing, aware of being non-beings, walling themselves off from life's potential to be proof against any further invasion and hurt.

There are the accommodating, fawning, cringing – who no longer make claims to an authentic life for themselves, but see hope in fitting successfully into the lives of others.

There are the downtrodden who yet retain their pride, defying the lowly estimation made of them by others, quietly or aggressively asserting their personal worth against all the odds.

There are those who begin to recover their dignity and to claim a worthier place in society by organizing their strength. They aim to secure a stake in decisions which affect their lives. They work to establish a form of communal power which is itself a statement that they matter.

There are the rich and powerful who voicelessly cry out as much as any for deliverance, wherever they have made material wealth and position their God.

This variety of forms of impoverishment presents the biblical text with difficult questions. For, clearly, the poor are not simply the economically deprived. When economic deprivation as such is intended in the Bible, a further word is added in the text to make this meaning clear. Why must we track down what essentially constitutes poverty in the sight of God? All through the Bible it is made evident that the poor are special objects of God's love. The place given to the poor by men is taken to be a gauge of the extent to which mankind gains God's approval or stands under his judgment. The poor confront other men as a continual question put by God to find out where each stands. Are fellow human beings being accorded God's valuation of their lives, or deprived of that? Where the latter is the case, it is a clear imperative of God's loving presence that the situation be remedied. The poor must be given the place which he demands for them, or the consequences suffered. They play too crucial a role in God's work to remain unidentified. So, then, who are the poor? Why are they specially loved by God? How is change in their situation to be brought about? What does this change mean for the world and for themselves (e.g. if they stop being poor do they stop being God's beloved and chosen?)?

The prophets declared God's judgment on those who reduced the poor to commodities to be bought and sold. They pointed to the sign this represented of a world turned aside from its purpose – which must recover direction through giving fresh heed to God's will for his world. The hinge of massive change is in Jesus Christ, who came in the likeness of a slave (Phil. 2.7). Though he was rich he became poor that, through his poverty, he might make others rich (II Cor. 8.9). His self-emptying has robbed brute power of its glamour, and points a new way.

On the basis of this life-pattern, it can be the poor who are truly rich (James 2.5). Churches which are impoverished may have greater wealth than those which enjoy plenty (e.g. the church in Smyrna, Rev. 2.9 compared with that in Laodicea in Rev. 3.17). The down-graded everywhere are given new status – tax gatherers and sinners are revalued in relation to the righteous (Luke 18.9-14), are offered a new life (Luke 19.1-10), inherit the kingdom (Matt. 21.31, 32). It is moral revolution.

God's beloved, God's chosen can only be recognized as such if there is another revolution – a revolution in perception: a readiness to discern and acknowledge worth in what had been treated as worthless. 'He has chosen things low and contemptible, mere nothings, to overthrow the existing order' (see I Cor. 1.25-31). 'The meek shall inherit the earth' (Matt. 5.5). 'Unless you turn round and become like children you will never enter the kingdom of Heaven' (Matt. 18.3).

But the question must be pressed home – who are the poor that

they are so beloved by God that he is so determined to prepare a
different destiny for them from the one which men are eager to
impose upon them?

The basic Hebrew and Greek words used in Old Testament
and New Testament are very similar in flavour. They have a
variety of application, but in all the variety, there are two con-
stants. The poor are (*a*) 'answering people' who are (*b*) made so by
means of a relationship forced upon them by others.

(*a*) The poor are those who are given no freedom to ask questions and make decisions: who can only make answer to the
questions and decisions levelled at them by others. Thus, in
Old Testament times, a king planning an embassage or going to
war, might line up his retainers and say 'I will send you, you and
you; and you, you and you will stay behind to look after things
for me here'. The retainers have no option except to answer to
plans already set out for them. All they can say is 'Yes, sir.' No
account is taken of their own preferences in the matter. They have
not opportunity to play a creative role. They are there to fit in
with the plans of others. Special people can choose their course and
drive ahead like ships. The 'bottom of the heap' people are in the
backwash of these choices, tossed here and there. Life is divided into
the decision-makers and the decision-sufferers. The poor suffer
decisions made for them by others, which take their lives right out
of their own hands.

The affront of this is that all human beings have been made in
the likeness of God. That likeness cannot by any stretch of the
imagination be evident where people are simply victims of the
way others choose to arrange life for them. That is rather to lose
what constitutes being human, being God's creation. To recover
this heritage, one has to be free to stand up like a man to circumstances – and to God himself, like Job. The cruel exposure
inflicted on the man born blind by Jesus in John 9, really amounted
to the provision of space for growth, so that he might cease to be
a victim, a beggar, and become a full man. As he learned to face
up to others and to life's demands with developing confidence,
self-awareness and capacity to make decisive choices, he came to
his stature. It was then that he stopped being poor. He was only
cured previously: now he was made whole. He stood before others
at last, not just a man with sight, but one who bore the marks
of God's likeness in his way of living life, one who could play a
part in God's purpose.

(*b*) It has suited many powerful groups through history to promote the view that it is part of the divine ordering of life that
some people are by nature decision-makers and others decision-
implementers. The biblical words make it clear that this is a mere

rationalization of enforced servitude. It is not by nature, nor is it for lack of merit that some people are the poor of the earth. They have been *made* into the poor of the earth, *by the action of others*. They are not by nature unfit to participate in actions which shape the future; they are *set aside* from them. They are not inferior people, they are *treated* as inferior. If righteousness is to be established on the earth – i.e. right dealings, right relationships, a world put right side up – then there is no alternative open to those who pray that God's kingdom may come on earth as in heaven, other than this: the poor must be restored to their true place in society. It is a point on which the future of the universe hangs.

Something here is of basic importance for the redistribution of income and opportunity within every country, and for aid and trade relationships between countries. The aim of any activity towards those who have been made poor – within any one society, or through the relationship imposed by one society upon another – must be essentially to help people to come alive so that they participate in shaping their own destinies. Welfare measures which leave people dependent, and forms of aid which turn people into passive receivers[1] will do nothing to attack the hard core of poverty as it is understood in the Bible. They are still the poor whose bodies are well-nourished but who leave their lives to trail after decisions made for them by others. If a people's material situation in the world is improved out of recognition and they are still left at the mercy of forces which control their lives from the outside, no word of deliverance has been spoken, God's judgment still remains heavy upon that situation.[2] To root out the poverty which affronts God entails bringing people alive. Nothing less. Jesus said he was come that mankind might have life and have it more abundantly. As all dictators, power-cliques and hierarchies know, the most disconcerting thing in the world is people who have come alive. It is a signal for the escalation of oppression. The menace Paulo Freire represented to the Brazilian authorities was not that he was in league with some movement which aimed to take over power. He was not. Something much more dangerous was happening. He was helping poor people to come alive.

So God wants us to take a dangerous road. He is bent on transforming every situation where man's initiative has been set aside and his humanity demeaned. His judgment is made known in the prophets – who not only declare it, but announce the presence of God in his world to bring about the needed changes. It is expressed decisively in the life, death and resurrection of Jesus Christ in whom God has overturned man's judgment. There is a new promise to life of which the Christian community should be a sign and foretaste, and which the human community must use as its compass and chart as it faces the different circumstances presented to it by history down the ages. To get such a new vision of this world is to touch the chords of grief and ecstasy in the human heart. Women who had that vision could see in a birth, for which there was no scientific evidence of importance, a world-shattering event. Statement was not enough. It had to be through poetry that the new world bursting through the old was celebrated. Thus we had Hannah's Song (I Sam. 2.1-10) and Mary's Song (Luke 1.46-55). It is not at all strange that, in our time, the griefs and expectations of the Third World are so often poured out in poetry. To understand the hurt to the universe caused by the setting-aside of the poor, and the new reality which has entered in Jesus Christ to change this situation, is to touch deep well-springs of the heart. Hannah sang 'In the Lord I now hold my head high'. It is the mark of a new human being. Mary sang: 'He has put down the mighty from their thrones and exalted those of low degree'. It is the mark of a new world.

Problems remain.

What of the rich who are poor? It is easier for a camel to pass through the eye of a needle than for them ('them' includes most of us who read this) to enter the kingdom. Yet with God all things are possible. What are the terms for the rich to find life? They must institute concrete change. They are called upon to act like Zacchaeus – to end the exploitive relationship from which they are benefiting and replace it with a just and generous relationship. In God's purpose, rich and poor have the same interest in arriving at a changed world order. It is in the interest of the rich as much as of the poor that the revolution which would give the poor their place should succeed. A world right side up will be a blessing to all. There is, accordingly, a strategic part to be played by the rich who are 'poor in spirit'. In personal life and national life they are to promote policies which will strip them of their kind of personal power and prestige and introduce servant-power in its place. They are to work for that change to take place. They have a crucial role as interpreters of that change, which is bound to be strenuously resisted.

In Britain, a slogan which came out of the Church Leaders' Conference in Selly Oak in the summer of 1972 was 'Live simply that others may simply live'. It has to be seriously questioned. Individuals, communities and whole societies may choose a more frugal form of living – and make no significant change in the terms of life. It is the will of God that the unequal terms of life be changed utterly. Nothing must divert us into more compassable options.

But the radical question remains. If such a change in the world is to be brought about so that the poor are given their place, how is it to be brought about?

One part of the answer seems to have to do with getting new ears and eyes instead of having 'fat' and 'heavy' ears and eyes – hardened and unperceptive ones. It seems to be a unanimous biblical testimony that, where the poor are crushed and offer no resistance, and where people's eyes get accustomed to seeing them in their abased state without any movement being made to change it, culpability is greatly increased. To see the evidence of judgment before one's eyes and to react with the hardening of the heart is to bring the judgment near. Where this happens, as in Amos 8.4-9, *the whole earth feels the effects*.

Through television and other forms of communication the plight of suffering people is now set vividly before our eyes. We need to perceive deeply the meaning of what we see (here is surely a role for the church today) or we will simply grow accustomed to horrors, harden our hearts and come under greater condemnation. There is also a biblical injunction to read the signs of the times. Wherever in the world one finds a new assertion of selfhood, of a life of significance on the part of classes and nations which had been downgraded, this is often interpreted as a menace to the stability of society. A significant work for the churches would be to teach people to hear, through the menace of the rising of peoples to claim their place in the sun, the promise of a worthier human society. Jesus' declaration in Luke 4.18-19 expresses this reality: the release and restoration of those who had been made to answer to the demands and requirements of others, *is here and now*. If Jesus' kingdom is a menace to an old order from which we have profited, we must learn to discard our selfishness and hear and receive the promise of God, now. We must help others to welcome thoroughgoing change.

We have still not come face to face with one of the crucial issues. In a time of liberation movements and guerilla warfare, it is not enough to say 'We have to grow new eyes and ears'. Even if that is fundamental – for without a change of perceptions and attitudes there will be no change in situations – we have to go on to ask how is it to take place? Will there need to be bloody engagements such as the world has never seen, before place is yielded up to the disinherited?

Nowhere in the Bible does there seem to be direct encouragement to the poor to take the law into their own hands. The poor man of the psalms is asked to look to God from whom will come his deliverance. The ways are unspecified, but the suggestion is that he must leave this to God. Prophets call upon rich exploiters to mend their ways and disgorge their riches. The situation is to be put right from the top. Those who wield power are to learn to wield it differently.

Mary, in the Magnificat, speaks of the poor being lifted high. But how this happens is not indicated. According to the text, it could happen like a volcanic eruption from the sea which throws up a new island, not previously on the map. It could happen outside man's action.

Christ was no Zealot.[3] Yet he, who is the poor man, is the New Man. As such, whether we like it or not, he took the law into his own hands. The violence which took place in Jerusalem and led to his crucifixion, was violence he incited by his deliberate confrontation of ecclesiastical and political orders. Peter and John were later to register the change made by his indwelling life by standing up to authorities and saying 'Is it right in God's eyes for us to obey you rather than God? Judge for yourselves. We cannot possibly give up speaking of things we have seen and heard' (Acts 4.18-20). Those who felt the power of a new spirit at work were impelled to act according to a new law. But Jesus and his disciples did not do this with active violence.

All through the New Testament there are indications that a new order is to replace the existing order – in this world, not only in the world to come. Likewise, there appears to be no suggestion that the disinherited are to bring this change to pass. What has this to say to revolutionary movements in our time?

The coming-of-age of humanity in this century is indicated in one respect by the growth of fascist regimes. People can no longer be kept in subjection by propaganda and promises. The full apparatus of brainwashing and of torture has to be deployed. Yet, in spite of this, it is notable how many pressures towards change have taken place through basically non-violent surges of the people. The ending of military rule in the Argentine through popular protest, however fragile the alternative, is a sign of the power which can be wielded by the powerless to bring down the powerful. Consider also the revolt of the people in Madagascar in 1972 and 1973; the march of thousands from San Miguelito on the establishment of the dictatorship in Panama in 1968 and after the death of Hector Gallego in 1971; the change in the character of government in Ethiopia and Portugal produced through the pressure of army and people in 1974; the overturning of the Greek Junta in the same year. A new power is abroad in the world – the power of self-assertion of peoples.

But still the question remains – *if there seems to be no alternative whatever*, is the violent overthrow of an oppressive regime a work to which the poor must put their hand in God's name?

What did Jesus mean when he said of his disciples who would

do what he himself was doing: 'he will do greater things still because I am going to the father' (John 14.12)? He must have been thinking about the effects of his mission which is now to the ends of the earth, to the end of time, penetrating all societies and hemispheres – in contrast to the 'straitening' to which he submitted, the geographical limitation of his own earthly life and mission. So this, at least, follows: our canvas must become 'Old Testament' in scope once more. It must deal with the rise and fall of kingdoms and peoples and the relation of these to the dynamic will of God. The 'greater things' surely must include the way in which the kingdoms of this world move towards becoming the kingdom.

But does this justify the use of violence to make change?

The exposition of scripture on this theme is being made in men's blood today. We are in a situation in which it is unprofitable to work at this theoretically, without asking how it is being worked out in practice. Too many, at a safe distance from positions in which agonizing choices have to be made, would like to decide for others how they should act. More light will come from asking how and why they *do* act as they do, in faith.

As far as the Christian community is concerned, the re-establishing of the poor in their rightful place in life is an essential part of the Christian's calling. It represents a response to God's loving will, a sign of the reality of his kingdom. The kingdom will come. Some are taking the path of violence as their response to that promise. They are aware of the evidence of dehumanizing qualities released by answering violence with violence. They take their chosen road with repentance and tears – and in fierce joy, to suffer for righteousness sake. Yet they take it. No less than repentance and tears are needed also by those who take the road of non-violent action. So often in the past, their stance has simply resulted in leaving the poor where they are, without a hand stretched out to deliver. What Christians in these seemingly contradictory vocations owe to one another is not finding 'one Christian line', theoretically. It is (*a*) acceptance of one another in one fellowship, without any form of excommunication, and (*b*) constant challenge to one another's decisions – made on the basis of a common faith. A Christian community worthy of the name must bring mutual acceptance and criticism to bear, and so work out the demands of love and justice in real terms related to real situations. No formula will cover different situations. What Christians can do is act and pray and bare their thoughts and deeds to one another.

The opposite of 'poverty' in Hebrew is not 'riches' but 'violence'. Either you are poor or you are violent! It is only slowly dawning, in our day, that if the poor are to be rehabilitated in society, institutionalized violence – i.e. violence built into the very fabric and habits of social relationships, war on man's humanity within a seemingly peaceful framework of life – has to be dealt with. Can violence be countered without force? In legal terms and in criminal proceedings, society has found it impossible to control violence without force. Is that which fights against the poor and keeps them ground down controllable without counter-force?

The economically poor are treated in the Bible as a disinherited *class*: if they come alive, class struggle, in a variety of forms, becomes a necessity, for the good of rich and poor alike. As the economically poor exist within a broader community of the poor, so class struggle must be undertaken in the broader context of the total liberation of man and be disciplined and controlled by that larger objective. Then it is responsible counter-force.

Early in 1972, before the coup, a Chilean bishop was asked about the relationship between the biblical message and contemporary political responsibilities in his society. That part of the interview went as follows:

A. Such a study of the Bible as I have done, such an understanding of history as I have had, makes it very clear to me that God *is* concerned for this world; that he *is* the Lord of history and not merely the Lord of the world beyond history. His kingdom is something which must be in some way manifested in the present world, in all its structures. To be sure, we are not promised in the Bible that this will happen in the present age, but as the call of the prophets of the Old Testament make so clear (Amos, Micah, Isaiah especially) and so much of the New Testament also (I think especially of the Magnificat and the words of Mary), it seems so clear that God expects justice in the present world. How is this to be achieved except through those who are sensitive to his will, therefore? How can Christians ignore the injustices of social and economic structures and still be faithful to the total message of the Bible?

Q. Do you think there is a clear instruction about commitment to society and to changes in society in the New Testament?
A. I have already cited the Song of Mary. There are passages in the New Testament that would seem to indicate a passive attitude towards authority, a respect for all authority. I think we have to remember that Paul, in counselling submission to authority, is speaking of the only alternative open to the Christians at that time. They had no possibility of sharing in political decisions. Ours is a world in which we *do*. Our situation is entirely different. Here is where we have to take the Lord's Prayer seriously, that God's will

may be done on earth as it is in heaven; and as Christian citizens, wherever there are democratic possibilities such as we have had in Chile, to use these political options to work for a more just social and economic order. In other words, the message of the Bible as a whole has to be taken, it seems to me. It places before us the following understanding of the Lordship of God in history – we now live at a moment in history when we are called to be active participants in the doing of God's will, not only in individual acts of charity but in creating structures of justice: for we now have the power to do so.

Q. Would a prophetic church be more likely to align itself with movements for revolutionary change in society at this time of history, do you think?

A. Unquestionably, yes – in my own mind. But, as we speak of revolutionary change, to many this may bring to mind a violent change with a high cost of life, disregard for the rights of those who have worked hard all their lives: 'revolutionary change' should certainly have a broader meaning than that. We mean radical change, a change in which the structures of society are ordered in such a way that those who have received the dregs, or those who have been completely at the margin of the benefits of the productive process, are also included. I believe that it is clear that it is God's will that none of his people be oppressed, that God's compassionate stance is towards all men – in such a way that it is against his will that some should have too much when others have nothing. If this means revolutionary change, then I do believe the Bible is for it.

Now that kind of revolution applies not only, of course, to change of structures but also to a new mentality. It is not a coincidence that Chile's new government has been calling for a new man, and specifically defining the new man as that person who is able and willing to think of the good of the whole and not only of his own good. Somehow we must move towards a society where people see to it that such terms and such structures are worked out, that they *do* operate for the good of the whole – of each and every one. Then I think we should be far closer to God's will for mankind than anything we have seen yet.

Q. Do you think that this emphasis on a new man as the great need of Chilean society is related to what the churches might offer from the gospel in terms of a new humanity?

A. Most definitely so. For me a key verse in the Bible, just as important as John 3.16 is II Corinthians 5.15: '[He died] that men ... should live no longer for themselves but for him who for their sakes died and was raised to life.' It would seem to me that the very essence of the gospel will be to create this change in man so that they shall no longer live for themselves, but for Christ. And what living for Christ means is perhaps clearest of all in Matthew 25, in the parable of the final judgment – 'inasmuch as you have rendered it to the least of these, you have rendered it to me.'

Q. That leads me straight to my next question – must the church at this time of history be, in a way that maybe it was meant to be in the past but now it simply has to be, and dare not be otherwise, the church of the poor?

A. Yes, I believe that is true. For certainly as we look at the world through the eyes of Jesus we look on the masses of disinherited and oppressed with his eyes of compassion. Therefore, the crucial test of whether the church is fulfilling Christ's will would be the way in which it is concerned for those who are the least, and the last, for those who have nothing. Perhaps here we should think not only of those who have nothing in terms of this world's goods, but who, because of their cultural economic deprivation, are living less than a human life. That does not mean we are not concerned for those who have perhaps a surfeit of the world's goods, who are also in great spiritual need, or perhaps are in a much greater spiritual need than those who are poor; but it seems that Christ – in the Bible – is especially drawn to those who have not had a chance to live even a decent human life. If we can reach these people with a liberating gospel and bring change to their life now as well as promise of a life hereafter in the fullness of Christ's presence, then we will be doing what Christ came to do when he called forth his disciples and called forth his church.

Q. Is a theology of liberation relevant?

A. Of course it is relevant. My problem with the term 'theology of liberation' is just how do we understand this liberation? If we understand it in a purely secular or elemental sense then it seems to me that it falls far short of what the gospel means by liberation. In the gospel we see that man's problem is so clearly his sinfulness, his need to be forgiven, and his need to find a new life and to make Christ the centre of his life. The liberation the gospel promises is for this life and the hereafter; it implies a personal change as well as social change. We can understand the theology of liberation in this sense. It is talking about the gospel – no more, no less.

What happens if the poor get the upper hand and lord it in their turn? They simply fall under the same judgment as those who once oppressed them. This needs to be thought of *in preparing* for revolution, not just *after* the revolution.

## 5 *The Claim of the World*

In official and unofficial statements, the church invites Christians to have a responsible relationship to the world in which they are set. Yet these statements often fail to reckon with a deep confusion. For, in practice, Christians are driven two ways.

On the one hand, they may have the feeling in their bones that you cannot live a responsible Christian life if you extract yourself from ordinary company and turn your back on ordinary customs and ways. Christians are to be 'in the situation', identified with other human beings, open to the pressures which fall on them, accepting the terms of life which are normal for most people. But then, if they take this line, their life seems to be indistinguishable from any other. It has no peculiarly Christian mark upon it. As far as anyone can see, they are just part of the crowd, falling in, conforming.

On the other hand, to try to make a clear and distinctive witness, to adopt a noticeably different style of life, seems to set Christians apart in an unnatural and perhaps self-righteous way, making the Christian community into a ghetto, separated from the rest of mankind so that it is in no position to be 'salt' or 'leaven' in the human community.

Instinctively most seem to feel that they must stay with their fellow men and accept the conditions which obtain for them – adopting habits and relationships which are simply good, human habits and relationships. All the time they may be wondering whether something more is not asked of them, some specifically Christian witness: whether they are not giving in to worldliness.

Scripture does not help them at all. Rather it is the source of their confusion. At one time it seems to say one thing quite clearly, at another time something quite different. Listen to what they hear and read.

The whole world lieth in the evil one. Friendship with the world is enmity with God. Love not the world neither the things that are in the world: if you love the world how can the love of the Father abide in you? Be not conformed to this world. The fashion of this world passes away. It was the rulers of this world who crucified the King of Glory. The Prince of this world is to be cast out. That sounds pretty decisive. Man has to choose between the church and the seducing world:

There will always be the Church and the world
and the soul of man
shivering and fluttering between them,
choosing and chosen,
valiant, ignoble, dark and full of light,
swinging between Hell-gate and Heaven-gate;
and the gates of Hell shall not prevail ...[4]

But then the scriptures come up with clear contradiction of this. God was in Christ reconciling the world to himself. God so loved the world that he gave his only begotten Son. God sent not his Son into the world to judge it but to save it. Testimony is to be given to Christ that the world may believe. Christ prayed that his disciples should not be taken out of the world. The kingdoms of this world are to become the kingdom of our Lord and of his Christ. Accordingly it was said at the Evaston Assembly: 'Without the gospel the world is without sense; without the world, the gospel is without reality.'

What seems to be a double voice from scripture may be examined in these passages: for the world as an order of being hostile to God and his purposes: John 12.31; 16.11; Rom. 12.2; I Cor. 2.8; II Cor. 4.4; Eph. 2.2; James 4.4; I John 2.15-17; 5.19. For the world as the object of God's redemptive love: John 3.16-17; 12.46-47; 17.21-26; I Cor. 5.9-10; II Cor. 5.17-19; I John 4.14; Rev. 4.11; 11.15; 21.1-5, 24-26.

In the Bible the word 'world', whether what is thought of is time-span (aeon) or space-habitation (cosmos), is used in at least four different senses.

World may indicate all that is not God and that has to be distinguished from him: everything that he has made, including man.

Next, man may be treated as standing representative for all creation. Its promise or frustration finds focus in his relationship to God, and is decided by the character of that relationship.

Thus, thirdly, 'world' may indicate an order become estranged, infected throughout by human sin, alienated from God and hostile to his purpose.

Lastly, 'world' may stand for a redeemed order, changed radically by the power of Christ's work, so that it is on the way to becoming that world on which God set his heart from the beginning.

Small wonder that ordinary church members give up.

Yet there is a simplicity about all this. We live in an order created good by God, summed up in man, estranged and redeemed. Let people get this straight and different nuances will become clear when they face particular passages of scripture. There is only one world we have to face. All that God has made, for which man stands representative, has fallen away from him to exercise a destructive pull, subtly centred on man's own self-will instead of on God: but Christ has dealt with this, broken the grip in his crucifixion, established himself as the one power that counts, and draws creation and man into a destiny in which all that they were cut out to be will be fully realized.

If this is so, there is not one form of worldliness but two. There is a worldliness to be shunned and a worldliness to be coveted.

The choice is not 'being found in all kinds of company, or "God's way", some alternative to such "worldliness" '; 'delighting in bodily feeling and expression/or "God's way" '; 'getting involved up to the elbows in the grime of political infighting/or "God's way" '. For too long men and women have been put on the rack by these false alternatives and have been subjected to bastard crucifixions. The Christian life is a full-blooded one. It is to be lived after the pattern of the man who was called glutton and wine-bibber, who lived life to the full and offered abundant life to others, who took the risks involved in confronting political and religious authorities in the name of truth. These different elements – the company one keeps, bodily aliveness, political commitment – simply provide *some of the terms* according to which life in Christ is to be worked out. They are not, as such, *set over against* life in Christ. When we look at the worldliness which is to be shunned it has a very different character from this simple '... either ... or ...' alternative, this black-and-white option.

First, it may be essentially a state of drift. The world is treated as meaningless, as going nowhere, a cork on the waves of time. God is not genuinely in charge, and one is not answerable to him. Life is to be dealt with casually and uncritically, letting things take their course. One floats, unresisting, in the currents of popular opinion. One's attitude to life is shaped by the particular slant of the newspaper taken off the news-stall, or by the advertising in the supermarket. Worldliness is, in one characteristic, irresponsibility.

Alternatively, worldliness may be marked by the dynamic of self-sufficiency. The great thing in this case is to get life to run the way you choose. Leave God out by denying him – or by professing him and keeping him just where you want him! Protect your interests, while making loud noises about the interests of others, to divert attention. Keep intact. The UNCTAD Conference in Chile was an exercise in worldliness of the worst kind on the part of the rich nations. There were noises of concern for the poor world, but the fundamental choices registered the blatant self-interest of the rich.

Worldliness, either as drift or as self-sufficiency, will certainly prove to be delusive. Where Jesus Christ is Lord, life will not work the way the 'shrug it off' or the 'bend it your way' approaches demand. Their advocates, accordingly, must protect themselves by illusion, by making their own little worlds which are designed to offer fulfilment for their own plans. These worlds of illusion become centres of resistance to Christ's will and purposes. History will find them out. But while they have their day, they will exercise a strong pull on human societies.

Over against these two forms of evil worldliness there is a genuine worldliness which is to be coveted. It accepts this material world as it is constituted, accepts human make-up as it is without blinkers, accepts the company of all sorts of men and women. This context, the world exactly as it really is, is taken to offer proper terms for Christian living. Men and nations who exercise this positive worldliness develop a response of imaginative stewardship for every created thing entrusted to mankind. They use it to share it, treating it as precious but not as their own possession. Material aid offered from the well-off countries to the poorer ones is always an expression of worldliness. But mostly it has been the expression of self-interest, the evil form of worldliness. What is wanted is not a departure from worldly concern, but a creative form of worldliness in its place.

You cannot escape being worldly.[5] It was said of Jesus Christ 'as he was so are we in this world'. We have no alternative to leading a life of worldliness. What we can choose is the kind of worldliness.

Wherever churches are drifting along from year to year, not stirring themselves – or hiding their essential irresponsibility beneath a veneer of self-justifying activity – they come into condemnation. Whenever Christians, whatever front they put up, have their minds and attitudes decided by the influences which fall on them from their environment, they come into condemnation (do they vote according to their income group like other materialists?).

Wherever a church is proud of its record (God help us), unperturbed by the suffering of Christians in countries which know oppression, wrapped up in its programmes and buildings, delighted that it has such superior doctrine, liturgy or form of ministry to point to, it is damned in the sight of God as worldly and delusive, fit for the burning. No wonder that publicans and harlots (note: not ex-publicans and ex-harlots, but practising publicans, practising harlots) go into the kingdom before the righteous. If you are knocked around, as a harlot is, a lot of your delusions may be knocked out of you, and you may develop a true touch.

The church needs to lead a servant life in the world because the world as world does not know its own nature and destiny. It does not know that Christ has conquered the powers which kept it enslaved, that he has opened a way to freedom. This must be shouted out by word and by deed, in joyful world-affirmation.

The fight is over and the fight is on.

## 6 *Principalities and Powers*

Great shaping forces, designed by man, are at work in the world. In some parts, forces not designed by man produce drought, flooding, earthquake, hurricane, and are still the forces to be feared. But more and more the menace of nature to man is yielding to the menace of man, using nature's forces, to man. Centres of power are built up which become hard to control.

Military machines represent concentrations of force, often backed by the use of an advanced technology, which afford enormous potential for destructiveness. If you have a beautiful weapon, it is hard to resist the temptation to give it a real-life try-out – to see if it does all that the manufacturers claim. Yet these concentrations of violence-in-waiting can be traced back to the original need to provide means for communal control of individual or group violence within societies, and constraint of violent aggression between nations.

The working of multinational companies has only lately been diagnosed as a force in world politics and economics which is inadequately controlled. With enormous capital resources behind them; with infiltration webs spread across the globe; with a certain freedom from any one country's laws due to the network of countries also implicated – they can apply pressures and remove pressures which may drastically affect the future of nations whose resources are insufficient or insufficiently organized to counter them. Their influence may be decisive for the rise and fall of kingdoms. Yet they also represent a promise. Enterprise which nations could not tackle individually can be tackled through the assembling of collective gifts and resources. Horizons of international action are suggested which could be for the healing and blessing of men.

The apparatus of any religion is a form of accumulated force. Its promoters can profess love of freedom while keeping devotees in subjection. As with the multinational company, this power can affect policies in lands in which it is strongly established using its international network and, through explicit concordats or unspoken agreements, can quite often influence the direction of major policies and alliances of countries. Yet the purpose for which the apparatus ostensibly exists is to secure fullness of life for the faithful, and, if the religion has a broader concern, for humankind.

Within nations, government is given authority to shape a nation's life to a large extent and to define its relationships to other nations. The church may be an influence in the land. There will also be lobbies and pressure groups which represent commercial, financial or labour interests, for instance – each concentrating a measure of force to influence policies which could favour or disfavour their concerns. There are institutions, organizations, movements which to a greater or lesser extent have a say in the way society will go. There are also tides of human aspiration and fashion which seem to be to a certain extent manipulated by men, but which develop their own rhythms and characteristics. All these are capable of producing an impact which can shape life substantially for good or ill. They are 'powers'.

In the scriptures, reference is made to identities familiarly listed as 'thrones, dominions, principalities, powers'. These words indicate mysterious, dominating forces which may get men and women in their grip, which could also exist for their blessing.

'Thrones, dominions, principalities, powers' bear these characteristics: (1) their existence indicates a hinterland beyond human life where good and bad spirits fight it out, with consequences for human life and destiny. (2) There is a clear tie-up with human sin: but it is not so much that human sin creates these powers as that it gives them the green light so that they have a chance to establish themselves and make their presence felt in their own way. (3) There is a relationship with nature, a suggestion that it provides them with one way of getting at man. (4) A compelling influence is exercised in everyday affairs through their articulation in institutionalized and routine forms, like government. (5) Their effect on human society may be felt like that of a river in flood: they can rise up suddenly, gain momentum, sweep people along, burst the banks of existing communities, shape life in a way that people do not consciously choose.

Though they have these characteristics, they are never pinned down in the Bible and given a recognizable origin. Ultimately they are left mysterious.

Since they have a commanding capacity to get human life into their clutches and human beings at their mercy, serious attention must be paid to the knowledge of them which can be gleaned from the Bible. These concentrations of force have (it is not clear whether this is quite universally so) an acknowledged place in God's original scheme of things: they have taken on a usurping character and seek to overturn Jesus Christ's purpose; he has dealt with them on the cross, reducing to tatters their pretensions; they were brought to heel in the resurrection; they now exist to serve him, and in the long run, have no option; they still show usurping tendencies and men may fall under their spell; but in the end, with the whole creation, they will serve Christ as Lord and King.

These powers and authorities had their good place in God's original purpose. They exist to serve his will (Rom. 13.1-4; Col. 1.16). They have a tie-up with the natural creation (Rev. 7.1-3). But they have sought to usurp Christ's place and then must be resisted (Eph. 2.1-3; 6.10-13; Rev. 13). We need not fear them or submit to them (Rom. 8.38-39) for Christ had dealt with them decisively both in their legalistic and eruptive manifestations (I Cor. 15.24-25; Col. 2.13-17, 20-23; 1 Peter 3.22; Heb. 2.8, 10-13).

These large-scale forces which play a part in the destiny of the creation, find expression also at a personal level. Jesus Christ delivered people from a grip on them which was other than their own grip and other than his. When he cast out demons and when he warned about the cleansed life into which seven other devils might enter, he was declaring his authority over alien and intruding forces which enslaved human beings who opened themselves to a grip on their life other than God's (Luke 11.24-26). In his acts of healing and restoration he exercised his authority to denounce the evil grip and announce God's saving grip on human situations.

In Gethsemane, when the disciples were so cruelly overpowered by sleep and Jesus was deprived of their concern and prayers, do we not see a natural force which has normally a healing, beneficial part to play becoming the very force which breaks companionship between the disciples and their Lord? Is not this characteristic of ways in which an influence may step in, so ordinary in life's routine that we are not alert to the danger of it, to disarm us so that, before we notice it, we fail and betray our Lord?

Before Pilate, Jesus asserted: 'You would have no authority at all except it were given you from above.' Jesus, by the very fact that he stands trial, illustrates that legitimate authority can be mishandled and abused. At the same point he affirms the proper place of such authority, which has its origin in God. When authorities have to be fronted it is not to dispense with lawful authority, but that authority may recover its true face. It is 'from above'.

When Jesus became sure that he must put all to the test in the last week of his life at Jerusalem he spent time teaching his disciples. Teaching them what? Teaching them to live in a situation dominated (to all appearances) by the principalities and powers. He taught them to live in a sweep of history which would buffet him, pulse with mounting terror, hurry him along to his death. He taught them that, however things looked, he would have the upper hand. They learned ill, and failed him. But, when the Holy Spirit took hold of them and made new men of them, persecution found them able to live and die in just such situations, enduring to the end in faith. This last week teaches men how to live out the prayer that God's kingdom may come and his will be done on earth as in heaven, in revolutionary situations. It is food for our time. It speaks of usurping powers tamed so that they may become a blessing instead of a curse. Yet the wrestling to control and direct these forces will bring from man sweat like great drops of blood, for he must contend with them as long as life will last.

## 7  *Sin, Wrath, Repentance*

Sin is that which, in the Bible, disrupts and distorts relationships – of man with God, with his fellow man and with the rest of the created order. A stronger emphasis is laid in the Bible on the damage done to social cohesion than on that done to individual or domestic integrity. More than anything else, sin is an affront to community relationships, a spoiling and thwarting of these, a twisting of them to evil ends. On a large canvas, sin stands for that which turns aside and twists out of recognition God's whole purpose for the community of mankind.

Jesus Christ did not spend time analysing sin's character and tracing its origins. He just dealt with it.

To put the word into its context and discover its meaning afresh, one would need to consider situations where good community relationships are seen to be of fundamental importance. We may look for light to the continent of Africa and to the young people of the world. Over the enormous range of cultures and languages to be found across the continent of Africa there seems to exist, on this matter, basic understanding. Sin is particularly the befouling of community life, the putting in disarray of positive forces which uphold society, the poisoning of healthy and supportive elements which bind people together. Where communities are racked by internal dissention or mistrust, and where their relationship to other communities is arrogant, ingratiating or demeaning, sin describes what has gone wrong.[6] In the Western world, by marches and protests and sit-ins, young people in many countries show an awareness of the responsibility human beings must exercise towards one another in the way they run their societies. They are often accused of lacking a sense of sin. The point of the charge lies in what are presumed to be their individual moral standards. But the sense of communal sin they show is something new in history. They are aware of the way in which a nation or a whole hemisphere can allow its relationships with other parts of the world to be twisted and distorted so that, under a fair face, unchecked exploitation proceeds. They are the bearers of a great hope. For history has indicated the difficulty of developing a communal sense of sin on the basis of an individual one. It may be possible to develop an awareness of sin's penetration of personal life on the basis of deep awareness of its social manifestations.[7]

In the prophetic witness of the Old Testament, 'remembrance of the covenant with God' is related to the need for an awareness of the sin (both within its life and in its relationship to other countries) which can mark a whole nation or group of nations. We must in our time ask how God's hand is to be seen in relationships between nations and hemispheres. We must learn to recognize, in the exploitation and degradation which nations force on one another, the flouting of God's will, the reign of sin and death.

Many facets of the words used for sin in the Bible find vivid expression in both personal and international relationships today. These include: missing the target at which humanity should aim; going astray from the path which humanity should take; unfaithfulness to agreements; the promotion of violence and destruction; the enthroning of worthlessness; the rejection of God's way, either openly or under a religious screen.

In such situations the wrath of God comes into effect. The sin of man goes against the grain of the universe, and man cannot escape the consequences.

The word 'anger' is used of God to indicate how deeply he feels and reacts to human sin. But the phrase 'wrath of God' should not conjure up a picture of a heavenly Father, who, provoked beyond endurance, lashes out at recalcitrant man. Rather it refers to the way the world is constituted. You cannot sow one thing and reap another. You cannot go against God's purpsoe for his world without planting deep in that world seeds of deprivation and despair which must one day be harvested. The harvesting is the revelation of God's wrath.

Oppression and torture will produce submission – but will also nourish rebels dedicated to bring about change, and will temper the spirit of martyrs.

Nation will exploit nation – but not without producing a slow-burning flame of resentment which one day may break out in a firestorm.

Watergates will take place. But there will also be Watergate hearings.[8]

If the whole nature of the universe is such that those who try to work it for their selfish purposes will face a day of reckoning, then what kind of day awaits those of us in the Northern Hemisphere who have for so long taken what belongs to the rest of the world and who still live on other men's goods and labour? If the universe is simply an order which ensures that human beings reap what they sow, then there is no way out of the trap which our history has laid for us.

If we take seriously the way that God must blaze with indignation at the desecration wrought on his beloved human family, *we may cry out to be destroyed*, rather than see him face to face with this sin upon us:

And there was a violent earthquake; the sun turned black as a funeral pall and the moon all red as blood; the stars in the sky fell to the earth, like figs shaken down by a gale; the sky vanished, as a scroll is rolled up, and every mountain and island was moved from its place. Then the kings of the earth, magnates and marshals, the rich and the powerful, and all men, slave or free, hid themselves in caves and mountain crags; and they called out to the mountains and the crags, 'fall on us, and hide us from the face of the One who sits on the throne and from the vengeance of the Lamb' (Rev. 6.12-16).

The saving thing is the reality of God's offer of repentance and forgiveness. This does not prevent human beings from having to face up to the consequences of their past deeds. Rather it allows these consequences to be borne redemptively. It produces a hope that humanity may break out of the old circle of injustice and bitter reaction to it. A Polish/East German group understood the meaning when they wrote: 'A start of new relationship ... is offered to us *despite* past history.'

Those who have lived at the expense of others must repent and believe the gospel. They must come under conviction of sin, deeply desire a change of life, throw themselves on God's mercy, receive forgiveness and amend relationships and practices. No one must forget the price at which this possibility was opened out to mankind. No one must underestimate the depth of the abyss of grief and self-loathing which marks the genuine road to repentance. We have very little skill as whole nations in humiliating ourselves before God, although we could pick up clues from the Old Testament. We are equally unskilled in discovering what amendment of life means in this one world – for hemispheres in their relationships to one another, for hierarchies, international combines and similar power blocs.

Those who would reach through repentance to amendment of life have to realize, as if it had never penetrated their defences before, the fact that God's judgment on earth is directly related to the raising up in status and place of those who have been made poor.

What stands in the way of repentance and forgiveness?

It is the will to acknowledge the wrong that has been done. But before that will can be activated, the nature and extent of the sufferings of others at our hands must penetrate mind, attitude, policies and pocket. One of the main roles which the church could play in the northern parts of the world is to help all men to *hear the reality experienced by those other parts which have been victims of northern policies*. The thick screen which has become a protective wall against awareness of what others are suffering became apparent in Europe when the first grants of the Programme to Combat Racism were announced. While African Christians[9] hailed this as a sign that the World Council of Churches was becoming genuinely a *World* Council of Churches, so many churches in Europe reacted defensively, and in an entirely different character from the history of their past complicity in the wars of their own nations. Without even evaluating the validity and appropriateness of such a commitment by the WCC, one can point out that the European reaction sprang from a base of European attitudes and interests, and involved practically no effort to listen to Christians who, accepting or rejecting violence, had at least to make their response of faith *in the situation*. Nor did it take account of the ending of violence in the Sudan, where the confidence that the WCC acted for Africans and not just for whites was a factor in helping the AACC and WCC to share in the peacemaking.

The screen must come down. A deep-going sense of shame and disgust is needed at the way in which so many peoples of the world have been made poor, denied initiative and creativity, compelled to fit in with the plans and policies of others, refused their dignity as human beings made in the image of God. There needs to develop an awareness of our own decisive part in producing and continuing such a situation. We must bare ourselves to the despairing resentment of the oppressed.

Words are not likely to have enough effect. We must hope that the wrath of God will operate in such a way that events will encourage us to come to our senses. It helps change in prodigals when the food runs out. The church may then be of service by interpreting positively signs of the times which otherwise might appear simply to be negative.

The exercise of power by oil-producing countries is more than simply an awkward event for oil-consuming peoples. Even though the riches go mainly into a small number of pockets, events afford us a sign that primary producer peoples need no longer be forced to have the terms of sale imposed upon them.[10] New confidence on the part of primary producers of minerals and perishables – so that they release their products in a controlled way which suits their own needs and economy and set up co-operative arrangements to make the most of the market – need to be interpreted as a promise of a better balance in the competitive jungle of international trade, and the heralding of greater possibilities of world community. In the same way, disturbances in British industry may point to the reality of a shift of power which offers the prospect of a more balanced distribution of wealth and a more genuine national community.[11]

If some of these signs of the times can be brought home to us so that it becomes clear that the world is not going to work on the old terms, that new community must be based on new terms – then there is some hope of an amendment of life on the part of nations which have lived off others.

To bring many nations to an awareness of the need for thorough-going repentance will be a massive job in itself. The power possessed by the poorer nations of the world is still very limited indeed. Signs and portents of alternative power appearing in Third World countries may not be sufficient in themselves to shake the rich world to the foundations. It may rest more than ever on the church to be the prophet of our time, drawing man's attention to the significance of these signs as offering an alternative path to the one which may lead to cataclysm produced by resentment and despair. The difficulty is all the greater since it is a very sophisticated thing to work out – for nations and for the complex institutions which make up the life of each nation – what repentance and amendment of life will mean. Pressure on firms to pay wages above subsistence level in South Africa and elsewhere and to reduce the gap between black and white workers' remuneration, pressures to withdraw investment which supports oppressive regimes – are the mere first signs of ways in which institutions might be helped towards repentance. Pressure on governments regarding alliances and arms sales offers one other possibility. A great deal of homework and hard work must be done. For it is not enough that individuals repent. There is no hope of a worthy human community without hemisphere repentance and amendment of life. Jesus Christ is not a 'household god' but Lord of all.

Principalities and powers, fallen away from their true calling and become agents of evil, already have, in Jesus Christ, one who can restore them to their true purpose. Those who believe in him must hear his calling and be found at his side, constraining the powers till they no longer thwart his will but serve it!

## 8  Renewal

Is the way of revolution the way of hope for the world? Or the way of reform? A great deal of play develops between these two words. Those who feel that radical change is needed in life tend to opt for the former word and dismiss the latter one as implying simply a patching up job. Repentance and amendment of life involve turning the whole world the other way up. Reform is just not enough.

Words which might be translated by 'revolution' or 'reform' are few and far between in the Bible. In Isaiah, Jeremiah and Hosea the words for 'revolution' or 'rebellion' are used for the rejection of the rule of God, not of man; and when, in the books of Kings and Chronicles the word is used in its modern understanding, it is neutral – simply recording the historical reaction of one people against another without making moral comment.[12] On the other hand, when the 'time of reformation' is mentioned in the Epistle to the Hebrews, what is indicated is a time of drastic change when everything will be made thoroughly right.[13]

Those who are conscious of the deepgoing change which will be needed in life if more effective signs of the kingdom are to appear in our time, prefer to use words like 'revolution' or 'radical reform'. In the Old Testament and New Testament, the same concern gathers round words for 'newness'. The presence of God the Father in his own world, the incarnation of Jesus Christ, the work of the Holy Spirit are presented as a new reality at the heart of the old which continually puts pressure on the old to become new and offers, in the end, the promise of new heavens and a new earth.

Then is 'renewal' what is asked of us today?

There are those who would put the emphasis on the 're' – and would assert that all that is suggested by the word is a dressing up of the old thing in new clothes, or some updating of it. For them, it seems to avoid the need for fundamental change. Others put the emphasis on the 'new' part. They look to the future and see the hope of an alternative order of life penetrating the present so that the past can be discarded. The hope is in unforeseen possibilities which lie ahead, which can alter radically the possibilities of life here and now. Others again put the emphasis on the transfer from the 're' to the 'new'. Things which had their place in life in past times are given quite new expression. They see, at one and the same time, an offer from God which preserves continuity with the past and which is yet quite transformed in its contemporary realization.

There are two main biblical words which we translate by the word 'new'. One refers to something which has just come on the

scene and was not there before. We would be using the word in
this sense if we said 'there are a lot of new shops in this area since
last I visited it'. The other word indicates something different in
quality. We would be using the word in this alternative sense if we
said 'the team has a new spirit in it, since it was threatened with
relegation'. It is in the latter sense that the word is used for matters
of spiritual renewal. What it points to is not novelty or strange
phenomenon – or something turning up out of the blue to save the
situation against all odds. What the word points to is rather the
capacity of God to produce a fundamental change in the present
so that new possibilities exist where older ones had seemed to be
determinative, and so that life has a quite different and hopeful
ring about it. This newness experienced in the present points
forward to a fulfilment in which human life will be caught up and
brought to its perfection (the new man will have a new song in his
mouth, will get a new name, will drink new wine in the New
Jerusalem).

Well, is the essential promise of the gospel that ancient things
will simply be put in a new form? Or is it that they will suffer a
drastic sea-change? Or is it that they will be discarded in favour
of exciting, fresh alternatives?

The first of these would produce nothing radically new, so
justice would not be done to the radical newness implied in the
biblical testimony to God's action.

The second and third set the ideas of continuity and discontinuity
against one another: and that is where the main difference lies
between those who want revolution and those who want reform of
church or society. St Paul's argument in I Cor. 15.35-49 emphasizes
that the new human order and the new humanity which are the
gift of Jesus Christ have a continuity with the old comparable to
that which a golden stem of grain has to the single seed disintegrated in the earth – it is new as something produced from the
sacrifice of the old. In contrast, the effect of the gospel is also
expressed in terms which suggest radical discontinuity with the old
– the new patch cannot be put on old cloth, nor the new wine in
old wineskins (Mark 2.21-28). St Paul elsewhere stresses the
dynamic of change inherent in life with Christ, the process of
becoming – the new humanity in Jesus Christ *is* already realized,
and *will be* spelt out through history (Eph. 2.14-22, 4.20-24; II Cor.
4.16; Col. 3.10): the dynamic of constant inward renewal means
that the old keeps being transformed and changed into what is set
out in gospel promises.

In the light of this, it is not too surprising that in the epistles of
John (1 John 2.7,8; 2 John 5) the commandment to love is both
old and new. In Jesus Christ what is old can only exist as newness.

A concrete example may clarify the situation. Jesus said that he did not come to destroy the law but to fulfil it. How did this strange assignment work out in practice?

It meant *discarding* the hallowed and well-tried – the Sabbath and circumcision, for instance, had to go.

Messiahship, on the other hand, was not discarded. Rather Jesus, coming as one who was poor, defenceless, vulnerable, the victim and yet the Anointed One of God, offered a *radical life-reinterpretation of messiahship*. Again: the whole scheme of temple sacrifice was gathered into his own death as the sacrificial lamb, so that it found a quite new expression which was both continuous and discontinuous with the old.

The resurrection was a breathtakingly unexpected *break-in of the new*. Possibilities which were simply not on the cards before, opened out. For instance, the inclusion of the Gentiles in the New Israel made the Law quite a different thing from what it had been before: and Paul wrestled bravely to reinterpret it.

Today, in the impact of the gospel on cultures which it had not previously been in contact with, one can find (among the healthy elements – there are unhealthy ones too) a destruction of the old, a dynamic transformation of the old, and a new which is so different one cannot see where it had any relationship to what had been there before.

There are hidden things waiting to be revealed (Isa. 42.9). It is not that they are not already in God's purpose. But they have been waiting for a *kairos* – the exactly appropriate moment to have full effect. Work God has been doing in the past will make quite a new impact when the hidden things are released into history. They may then appear to be out of place, alien to the church's real faith and task. They will be interpreted by many as the work of anti-Christ. The surprisingly new will be feared and resented by many, including those who are of the household of faith.[14]

Jesus said 'Greater things than these shall ye do, because I go to the Father'. Are these 'greater things' to replace his work, or to evidence it and thrust it home in new and startling ways?

When it says in the Book of Revelation 'the kingdoms of this world *are become* the Kingdom of our Lord and of his Christ' (not that the kingdoms of this world are set aside and replaced by the kingdom) the hope is that the totally new will have familiar features and show continuity with what preceeded it. The same hope is expressed in the resurrection of the body.

We get caught in a linguistic and intellectual trap if we insist on making continuity and discontinuity mutually exclusive alternatives. The Bible presents them in relationship. In the concrete struggles in which Christians must engage, to change the church and world in the direction of God's promise, they cannot expect to evidence all the aspects of 'the new' in the fullness in which these were evidenced by the whole man, Jesus Christ. But 'the new' beckons and commands. As he was, so are we to be in this world, this world made new continually by his presence, renewed daily by our participation in his work.

## 9    The Coming of Salvation

The crucial importance of space for many communities seeking a new life in the world, reflects back on the meaning of salvation in the Bible.

To have access to different physical possibilities may provide scope for the liberation of the spirit.

For the San Miguelito Community in Panama in their previous deprived situation, the church had seemed to be irrelevant or simply on the side of their oppressors. When they had means of making a life of their own, they found they needed a larger purpose on which to found that life, and so began to discover new possibilities in the Christian faith. A priest described the movement from constriction and depression into 'an open place', as the psalmist would put it (Ps. 18.19), thus: 'people had a sense of adventure, of spirit and faith in what they could become somewhere else. It was a sort of exodus for them …' Once they had the chance to settle down as a community and find direction for their lives, the same priest described 'ministry coming right out of the people, the desire to serve, the desire to support, the desire to give hope, the desire to help faith to grow – coming out of people who had never believed in any one or any thing in their lives'. Break out from the fenced-in life – the spirit gets a chance to grow.

A poor community on the outskirts of San José, Costa Rica, who also moved out to take over territory which was not theirs, building their shacks on both sides of a polluted stream, spoke of their sense of having been trapped in their previous situation – by low incomes, high rents, soaring prices, a hand-to-mouth existence with complete uncertainty about whether they would get any work and whether any such work would be reasonably paid. What gave them new horizons? Together they had made a decision to move; had organized themselves; had undertaken and carried through common action; had helped one another to erect their rough dwellings. The search for space in which to be human, to control their own lives and live them their own way – even if that was still in poor circumstances – had made them a real community. They knew they were better-off than many in better-off homes.

The Tondo people of Manila, the Philippines, represented a movement of thousands upon thousands into land over which they had no title – in order simply to have a chance to live. In spite of their continuing poverty, they have the look of people who are in charge of their own lives.

Aboriginals in Australia, opposing ranching and mining companies to reclaim their tribal lands are seeking something deeper than the repossession of territory. They are searching for room to re-establish their identity so that it is not some side-kick of the white man's identity, valued in terms of the white man's civilization. There are sacred lands which provide the cultural and religious nourishment of their own traditions. To break out from their low place in a white society into a place which allows them to lead authentic lives is for them a road of salvation, whether this is understood in a Christian sense or not; and it demands a different relationship to land; it demands spaciousness in which to grow.

Probably the biggest theological issue in the world is peoples' title to land which is theirs. It has to do with their identity and destiny in God's sight and man's.

The Turkana tribe, in Northern Kenya, suffering from drought and from war with raiding neighbours, found their cattle-based economy in ruins. What they needed to offer the prospect of new life was some alternative economic outlet. Through the good offices of the National Council of Churches of Kenya a fishing community of about 1,000 families was established successfully on the shores of Lake Rudolf. With the opening up of an alternative source of money, the society became more open to prostitution and materialism (fish were not sold to protein-deficient neighbours across the lake but to the Congo where higher prices could be obtained). A technical adviser, who had spent some months with the tribe, was asked whether the change had turned out to be in any way creative. 'Undoubtedly, in spite of all the disadvantages', he replied. 'The tribe is not much more than a loosely-integrated series of groupings, held together by self-interest. The fishing of the lake demands more: the work simply has to be done on a co-operative basis, using the finance, skills, and forms of leadership that different people can contribute. This is a break-out, a challenge to form a community on quite a different basis from the old one, on voluntary agreement and joint initiative.'

In a South African bantusan, the space which proved to be important was space for people to make decisions in their own time and in their own way. The black archdeacon of a community which had been forcibly expelled from their homes and left to start again from scratch in the veldt, became convinced that they needed a medical clinic. He knew of a European source which could be approached to provide the money. But he chose not to ask for it. Instead, as he moved among his people, he raised questions about their health and the health of their children, in the course of conversation. For a year nothing much happened. Then a few people came to him and said that they, the people of the township, felt that the medical care provided for them was inadequate. They would like to see what could be done to improve it. The archdeacon suggested they might discuss it with the elders, and this was agreed. The elders responded positively, and a meeting was arranged with the chief. All agreed that a medical clinic was needed and should be established. But how to go about turning the idea into reality? The people themselves volunteered to start a common fund, making extra articles for sale, growing a few extra vegetables. They had difficulty in scraping a living from the small pieces of land, with the men away in the cities – but after two and a half years they had raised about $100, a significant amount in relation to their income. Whatever was done from that point, even if outside money came in to meet the main part of the cost, the clinic would be something which belonged to them. What the archdeacon had provided for them was enough elbow-room to move towards an agreed judgment, and an agreed form of action to bring it into effect. This was not without loss. The time people took to come to a common mind meant that those who might have been cured suffered ill health over three years. On the other hand, once the community discovered its own mind and its own strength, it forged ahead. Before the clinic even appeared over the horizon, people were examining more critically possibilities of getting a better return from the land and of using the services of the agricultural adviser more effectively. They had become a people who had broken out from stagnation.

The basic meaning of the principal Old Testament word which we translate salvation, health or wholeness – and the New Testament one has a similar flavour – is to make spacious, be roomy, give outlet and freedom. A saviour is not someone who takes you, locked in your own hopeless situation, and removes you so that you can be locked into his promising one – but someone who opens a door to let you escape and live your life. To receive salvation is to have this freedom – it is not an encouragement to inertia ('after all, I am saved') but a call to responsibility. Those who have new freedom have room to exercise their human capacities. Pope Shenouda of the Coptic Orthodox Church once spoke about the coming of new life as being like the influence of rain on a plant or a bulb which has lain through the winter. The rain helps it to stir and grow; but is effective only if it helps it to grow *as itself*.

The opposite of salvation is not so much lostness as a sense of constriction and suffocation, of being hemmed in. So the Pharisees were concerned to walk in the way of salvation: but because they, by their practices, shut up the kingdom and neither went in themselves nor let others go in (Matt. 23.13) they fenced themselves off from the very salvation they sought. Religion which does not let one breathe, which does not let one be oneself, cannot derive from salvation in Christ.

The boundaries of the church are no longer nearly as visible as they were. All over the world, many movements and groups of Christians, who have been personally suffocated within the church institution and have been denied manoeuvring space, have found that to take the way of salvation for themselves and others meant to break clear. If God is Saviour, the last thing he wants is man gagged and bound and handed over, helpless, to himself.

Since God chooses to have a relationship with mankind such that each human person is not just an 'answering being' but a potential free partner in the renewal of the world, the idea of affording space to human beings is closely related to the possibility of their free participation in God's saving activity. The creative deliverance which dominates the Old Testament is the Exodus – the finding of a road out from slavery in Egypt. The focal point of the New Testament was described by Jesus himself as the exodus he was to accomplish at Jerusalem – this road out being not only for one enslaved people but for the whole of alienated humanity. At Pentecost a movement was initiated from the limited geographical space of Jesus' ministry to the ends of the earth, from his own chosen humble status to his 'filling all things', from the kingdom as a grain of mustard seed to the kingdom as a great tree, from the church as a new birth to the church as a community united in faith and knowledge of the Son of God growing up to become 'perfect Man, fully mature with the fullness of Christ himself' (Eph. 4.10-13). All life is to undergo change, and all human beings are to participate in this – not change for its own sake, but change towards the life God holds in store for the whole human race. If human beings are to move without constraint into this process of salvation and grow in it, then breathing-space, thinking-space, living-space, space for free movement and choice is crucial.

'Oppression' is almost the exact opposite of 'salvation' in the Bible. Jesus set himself alongside the oppressed when he became 'like a slave'. The word does not simply indicate deprivation of status and rights, but restriction of freedom to manoeuvre. In the crowning week of his life Jesus set himself at the mercy of the world's forces, fenced in, harried to his cross: 'I have a baptism to undergo, and what constraint I am under until the ordeal is over'

(Luke 12.50). His acceptance of geographical and vocational constriction has set us in a large place.

Further, like the word for the 'poor', the word 'salvation' has
to do with personal relationships. The hemming-in from which
humanity needs to escape is not caused by accident or by fate but
by the actions of others. Some human beings deny others room
to live.

Jesus Christ's victory over the powers which would hold mankind
captive was itself the provision of space which made possible risks,
ventures and achievements which the mighty had previously
declared out of bounds to the poor (such as his disciples were).
Now that the fences are down, mankind is meant to move out,
overcoming all oppressive powers, and the church is meant to be
a sign and a spur towards that goal.

Those who are unfree, cramped, without room to manoeuvre or
liberty to shape their lives for themselves, cornered and helpless,
are denied their basic human status and calling. Salvation is related
to the provision of a door of escape, and, through it, ground on
which they can walk as a people free to participate in making their
own future. They have, of course, still to be on guard. Powers
which seek to hold them enslaved may change their form, and still
dominate by means which look as if they were serving instead of
oppressing.[15]

State and church authorities alike feel insecure when people have
free space. It is instinctive in higher authorities to want to dominate; or, if they are milder, to domesticate in a fatherly way; or if
they even give that up, to keep the situation as tidy and manageable
as possible. The real danger is in giving people room. 'God knows
how sinful humanity may abuse such an uncontrolled field of possibilities' thinks the authoritarian side of sinful humanity. 'All
right if the room they claim were used to challenge the things we
want to challenge – but there is no guarantee whatever that, once
these have been challenged, the things we hold sacred and un-
assailable will not be challenged as well.' They are right. Nothing
is more awkward than an awakened people. There is no possibility
of keeping the expenditure of their energy and imagination to safe
channels once it has begun to flow.

God himself takes such a risk. He chooses not to breathe down
man's neck, but to be invisible. That is, he stands back from man to
provide a saving interval so that man's response to him is genuine
and free, not produced by the weight of his authority irresistibly
imposed. He removes himself, as an overwhelming presence. Then
man can know him in his presence as grace, instead of as terror.
At the same time, man is left much freer not to acknowledge him
at all. The Father chooses such freedom for his sons.

Jesus Christ removes himself from the human scene at the ascension in order to make space for the gracious work of the Holy Spirit. Philippians 2 emphasizes that even Christ's life is not a model we are to copy: what is desirable is that our lives should 'arise out of' that life, and that we get down to the task of working out our own salvation in fear and trembling. He leaves us free space to develop in, not a blueprint to copy.

The Bible loses all its vitality when it is made into a collection of proof texts, immediately applicable – that is, when there is no free play between the issues we face and the scriptural words and situations from which the Word may break forth. Words from the Bible do not necessarily correspond clearly to problems we want to refer to it. They may respond by producing confusion, throwing us back on deeper questions. They may reveal to us that we do not have an important problem. They may point us to joy, and reverse our preoccupation. We prowl, fascinated, round the scriptures like a dog round a porcupine, half expecting an encounter which may lift and energize us, half fearful of that unknown which may scare the living daylights out of us, shattering the world of understanding within which we had felt our faith was safe and secure, setting us, yelping, on the open road of salvation again.

If church or state would be instruments of salvation for humanity, their actions too must 'arise out of' the way God took with men. They must not be 'instead of' organizations, their leaders taking decisions and developing policies on their own, and then hoping to sell them to the people. They must be space-providing organizations, enabling human communities to develop in the most authentic way, even if that threatens their own position and security. They are to be agents of salvation, nothing less.

## 10   The Blessing of Man

What should the essential character of the church be at this point of history? Should it be a political church? Or a praying church? Or a servant church to meet social needs?

All that it is called to be at this point of history might find focus in the word 'blessing'. The church is to bless men, and be a blessing to men, and teach men to bless God. The word may seem to have a weak ring. But from its Old Testament root it has a strong resonance.

The word 'blessing' in Old and New Testaments is directly related to God's activity. God alone is the one who knows how to offer mankind blessing. Any hope men may have of relating themselves to one another and acting towards one another so that blessing is given and received, depends on this – that they set themselves humbly within the activity of God, and are true to the nature of that activity. Their assignment might be principally a work of contemplation or principally a work of political involvement, or a work which leads directly from one into the other – as in the case of Isaiah the prophet and statesman (Isa. 6). As far as they can understand the leading of God, some Christians may believe they have a *basic* vocation to pray, and others to engage in guerilla warfare, at this point of history.

Both kinds of presumed vocation are put in context and tested for faithfulness when it is asked whether they are a means of extending God's blessing to mankind. Prayer, as such, need not be an expression of faithfulness – it can be an escape from commitment, a form of evil worldliness. Participation in guerilla warfare may be an act of response to a loving God – or rejection of that love. Both may be short-sighted and faithless activities. They are nothing in themselves. In the introduction to his selected volume of Tennyson's poems, W. H. Auden having identified Tennyson as a lyric poet, perceptively asks what a lyric poet does when the mood is not on him; and answers that Tennyson had not the wit to think of any alternative, but went on writing, which accounts for so much bad poetry. He goes on: 'Trash is the inevitable result whenever a person tries to do for himself or for others by the writing of poetry what can only be done in some other way, by action, or study, or prayer.' What matters is finding what God calls us to, within his total activity of blessing his creation. Poetry which has no place in that activity is word-trash, action which has no place is action-trash, study is study-trash, and prayer prayer-trash.

Since God's loving outreach determines what will restore and enrich human life, rather than merely what he chooses to channel through the church, Christians will make themselves available to be means of blessing without monopolizing. They will work with all who may come within range of that outreach – atheists, agnostics, people of all faiths. Christians, as such, have no access to valid means of determining the worth of the responses of others. They must be humble before these (remembering the overturning of human verdicts in the parable of the last judgment Matt. 25). They must bring all they do themselves to the bar of God's judgment. There they will find again and again that the kingdom is bigger than the church. All kinds of people who would not be aware of it themselves, all kinds of activity which might not be immediately identified as Christian, prove to be signs of God's hand stretched out upon his human family. The church must not see itself as the only agent of God's blessing. God can choose whom he will – and, often in history, has not only chosen outside the church but has recalled the church to its true vocation by his activity outside its ranks. Yet the church does represent uniquely all the agents he may employ – wherever it becomes what it really is. It is to be a kind of 'first fruits', a first gathering of that promise which he holds in store for all human life. It is to be a pioneer of a new world. The church must concentrate on God and the world, aware of the needs of the world before God and available as a means whereby God may stretch out his hand over the world in renewing love. Where it acts as God's agent most humbly and decisively, it will get no kudos, no status. Its reward may be not even to be noticed (but how anxious it is to be noticed!). This will be in line with the gospel command: 'Let your light so shine before men that they may see your good works and *glorify your father who is in heaven*' (Matt. 5.16). A church which wants recognition for the good it does, begins to concentrate on itself: and that is its death, and the removal of a means of blessing provided for mankind.

The bestowal of blessing is an event, not just an idea or a wish. What goes out, goes out beyond recall and does a transforming work. Truly to bless human beings is to change their situation. It is to bring into that situation what was not there before, so that the factors which previously dominated it are put into a different relationship and perspective. There is no blessing where there is no concrete change. When Jacob tricked his brother Esau out of the blessing, it is as if something passed through Joseph which had gone beyond recall once it was released into another life. Some critics and commentators see in this story the remains of the influence of magic. But when Jesus blessed people, that also brought into their situation a new and decisive power. When he laid hands on the sick, it was not to wish them well but to cure them and restore them to a full life. If the church is to be a blessing to mankind, this can only come about if it brings into a situation those things which will change that situation into one which belongs to the new order of God's promise. Wherever that which can transform the enslaving reality in which people find themselves, is not brought to bear, there is no real blessing but only some phoney substitute. The church which is committed to being a blessing to mankind is committed to concrete change.

The blessing of individuals in the Bible has received most attention. But from the beginning of recorded history the promise of blessing was related to nations (Gen. 12.2,3 – God's blessing clearly is to be extended to families or nations, whether the wording implies that this comes through Abraham, or simply through a response similar to his). If nation is to be a blessing to nation and hemisphere to hemisphere, that implies the setting in motion of a delivering activity towards those in the world who have been deprived of dignity or status or hope. It demands a concrete change in the material terms on which relationships are based.

The complete absence of paternalism in the biblical word is worth noting. The agent of blessing is not to expect the receiver to become, through blessing, the kind of person, group or nation of which he could approve. That is irrelevant or worse. The effect of his own extending of blessing might be the opposite of what he might want. The receiver, too, is not blessed in order that his existing desires might be realized. He might have a very different road to take from the one he would instinctively choose. The entering in of this power of God into men and nations effects their release into their own particular fullness, as a gift of God for the blessing of all men, and the true expression of that fullness.

The relationship between richer and poorer nations in our day can be seen to be a blessed or cursed one by applying the measuring rod: Does what is extended from one to the other produce a situation of dependence? Does it seek to fit the possibilities which lie open to 'the blessed' into the plans and purposes of those who look upon themselves as 'bestowers'? If so, what is given is not blessing but an evil substitute.

How can those who are chosen to be agents of blessing know that they are really effecting the release of authentic life in others, instead of subtly using them in some way for their own ends? The sign of being blessed, as Dr J. Miguez Bonino pointed out (see above, p. 26), may be to become more awkward to deal with! The basis of this may lie in the conviction (1) that what the donor has to give has most often been made possible only by international robbery, (2) in the Christian community sharing should be normal and not need to be remarked on, (3) sharing which produces dependence is phoney. The Peruvian bakery co-operative (see above, p. 10), interpreted any external support they might be given as '... the proper returning to our land of some of the riches of which, for centuries, we have been despoiled.' Thus people who were hungry and without resources were very choosy about the quarter from which they were prepared to take money – continuing poverty was to be preferred to money which came bringing with it patronage or manipulation. The WCC Christian Aid Department showed itself to be a true agent of blessing in (a) giving the needed money without strings attached and (b) not being thanked and not asking to be thanked. When I obtained some money to help train an agronomist in the north of the Dominican Republic, I was not even told the money had been received. 'It is because acknowledgment might look like thanks' said a Dominican. 'They argue, "He is rich and we are poor. We are in the same community of Christ. Sharing should be normal and not need special acknowledgment." '

There is relevance here for work in the field of development. There must be a serious search to ensure that those who provide money, techniques, skills, personnel are not treated as patrons or benefactors; and that those who are receivers are not subtly forced to conform to imported ambitions and adapt to an external reading of their situation.[16] If development is to be a process of blessing in the biblical sense, it will be a means of discovering how life may sprout in new ways and still retain its own identity, in all the different soils of the world. It needs but a short step beyond this to recognize that the release of man's potential has to do with his *fruitfulness for others* ('that you may bear fruit in plenty ...' John 15.8). Once restoration takes place, the need of other human beings and institutions and nations for restoration becomes a calling to bless as one is blessed. The blessing extended is never for self-retention or for self-aggrandizement: but for self-giving. It was not enough for Jesus to put sick people on their feet, and make them well again. He made them whole, i.e. he made them people who could give themselves to God's total enterprise of transforming the world. To be blessed allows one to become part of an action of blessing which ripples out to the ends of the earth and the end of time.

The whole thing is personal. Any machinery or organization employed must be the means of, not a substitute for, human self-giving: just as skin, flesh and bone play their part when hands are laid on a person's head, to bestow what comes from the person of the Godhead. (To take one instance, if the World Council of Churches is to be an instrument of blessing those who, in its name, make contact with people in different countries, must do so not simply at an official level but at a deep personal level, as pastors, as human beings who care deeply for human beings.)

In response, man is to bless God. Commentators and critics say this cannot mean that man bestows anything on God. God needs nothing from man. Blessing, therefore, should, in this case, be interpreted as praise. This must be questioned. If from a full heart with the force of his whole being man blesses God does not God become blessed? Of course the resources made available through blessing are not in man's power but in God's own power – but if men, receiving these, offer them back in glad abandonment, is God not enriched? When mankind blesses God does this not help to make God complete – as the one who not only is who he is, but is acknowledged to be who he is by those he has chosen to be his free partners in a majestic enterprise?

## 11   *The Character of Ministry*

If the people of God keep their nerve, hierarchies have had their day. Bureaucracies which fulfil much the same role attend the same fate. The people of God have come of age. They must fulfil their responsibilities as adults, and reject every form of church government which would keep them children. The hierarchical type of organization belongs to the time of ignorance which God winked at. Now he calls on all men to repent.

Of course there are hierarchies and hierarchies. Are there some which effectively release the people of God into their joyful task? The shape of ministry in the Orthodox churches must be taken with new seriousness as a possible resource – although the service of the hierarchy in releasing the full potential of the people of God is not so obvious to outsiders as it seems to be to Orthodox hierarchies themselves! The point remains – if the people of God are *released* by a form of leadership we are no longer justified in calling that a hierarchy. For hierarchy indicates a sacred caste group who bear rule over others and make decisions for them. Among the defects which attend the hierarchical system of government are these:

(*a*) Their very structures encourage them to become, almost inevitably, 'instead of' organizations. They have a separate identity and prestige. This offers the possibility of acting 'for the good of' others, rather than with them.

(*b*) They are power-groups. They are wide open to the abuse of power to protect their own interests and their own positions. Wherever you find hierarchies you find manipulation, restrictive practices, administrative and financial pressures. They can isolate and relocate disturbers of their peace to defuse 'dangerous' situations. One must, however, go on to ask what kind of power they hold and exercise. Only in a limited number of instances is it brute secular power (an estimate from a reliable source places the capital invested by the Roman Catholic Church in Italian industry at one third of the total). The most dominating institutional church leadership has no apparatus which is the equivalent today of the Inquisition, no contemporary machinery to be compared with police terror and torture. There is always space which people of courage can use if they screw their courage to the sticking point. The problem of the power exercised is rather the attempted control of initiatives or the requirement that initiatives be referred for clearance – a power of the keys, to open things out or shut things down. In Britain, perhaps in Europe, the sins of politeness and diffidence have very often allowed the ordained leadership unilaterally to block or encourage promising developments (the appointment of one unsympathetic bishop effectively took the dynamic out of the Sheffield Industrial Mission).

(*c*) They are male and cannot represent the church.

(*d*) They seem to be constitutionally quite incapable of taking a John the Baptist attitude to new, emerging leadership: '... as he grows greater, I must grow less' (John 3.30). Their general characteristic is to inhibit, not to free into service the emerging qualities and gifts of the whole people of God.

This is not true everywhere. Bishop Ah Mya from Rangoon, said in a message to his people: 'In the newly-born province of Burma, what we need most is leadership. We need leaders who possess the quality and secret of teamwork, leaders who can quickly spot forces that are good and positive and can mobilize them for the whole Province. Not leaders who feel that they must lead, but leaders who feel that they must so serve as to produce leaders.' In an interview, Pope Shenouda of the Coptic Orthodox Church remarked: 'Authority in the church is a form of the exercise of love, trust and simplicity ... in any gathering of Christians, truth must preside not status: then clergy and laity can each exercise their proper authority.' It cannot be said, over the piece, looking back on history, that hierarchies have shown any great capacity 'so to serve as to produce leaders'. Emerging leadership has rarely been something to be welcomed. Rather it has been a threat to magisterial authority; or it has been regarded as presenting an area of confusion and untidiness in the church which would be better to be sorted out and regulated from the top. There is still enough space in most churches for alternative leadership to emerge and make impact. But if the leadership at 'the top' exists to encourage the development of multiple leadership at the base, then hierarchies seem to be quite the wrong instrument.

(*e*) The death seal set on hierarchies is in their non-disposable character. Over the centuries they have assumed a divine validation in themselves – which means that they are not subject to the mind of the people of God when their inadequacies cry out for remedy. They leave enough space to be bypassed, and that is happening all over the world, especially where latinized rather than eastern forms of hierarchies exist. But one must ask whether it is good enough that the overt leadership of the church be set aside or disregarded in order that the covert leadership might help the church to get on with the job. Signs of the times point the need for a leadership which can keep step with the maturing church.

(*f*) The main charge against hierarchies must be that they cannot do what the church needs, to grow up and move outward in love. The habit of trying to make decisions at the top and then filter them down is endemic. Mission cannot start from the top any more than a plant can grow from the flower down.

The action of a man like Dom Helder Camara and his leadership in the hierarchy in the Recife area of Brazil may offer fresh encouragement for the future of this form of church government. But he and those who join with him still form only a very small and unrepresentative proportion of the official leadership in Brazil. A few swallows do not make a summer.

Yet – if everything that is well-rooted starts from the ground, why talk about the need for leadership at all? Cannot God be trusted to raise up whom he chooses, as he raised up the judges in the Old Testament, to provide the kind of leadership that each situation requires? The judges themselves illustrate the weakness of *ad hoc* leadership. By the time we come to the New Testament, it is clear that God has made a more solid and continuous provision for building up his church. But does this mean some body which can act as a power in itself?

The search must be on continually for structures which release the Christian community into movement instead of impeding that community. The only authority which is likely to be acceptable at all today is authority which can authenticate itself as fulfilling a necessary part in forwarding the work of God in the world. Does the Bible give clues about 'releasing structures of ministry' and 'liberating forms of authority'?

Biblically, the word used for matters like 'church order', 'ordination' is a word of deployment.

The ascension of Jesus Christ was not a handover to consecrated men and women. It was the breaking out from its geographical restriction of the ministry Christ once exercised in the incarnation, to the ends of the earth and the end of time. The work of ministry or service is undertaken by Christ alive in the world; and ministry on the part of his people is a sharing in his work and an availability for whatever part he allocates. The gifts of the Spirit are distributed among the whole people.[17] They result in ministries some of which are 'emerging' and are relevant for limited periods, some of which are 'continuing'. The evidence of the New Testament is sometimes dismissed as being too varied and contradictory to give guidance regarding the ordering of ministry today. I believe it to be determinative. It is there quite clear that those who are chosen by God for particular assignments and have this recognized by the Christian community are set apart *for as long as a particular job is committed to them.* It is often not at all clear at the beginning whether the assignment is short-term or long-term – it may be for a large missionary journey, or just the next stage of a journey, or for something like a lifelong parish ministry. No basis can be found for the 'indelible laundry mark' theory – that once the sign is on you it is on you for life. You will not know, when you are set aside, nor will the church know at that point, in what way the commitment to play a particular part in God's overall strategy will work out.

We come back to the biblical basis. The Greek word is a word for the flexible undertaking of an assignment. Taken into a full Christian context, it points to the battles which have to be fought at different points in history by those who are concerned for the coming of the kingdom. It is a word for the march through life of people alert for the engagement of the enemy at any point. When the need for engagement appears, forces break from line of march to be deployed in line of battle. That is what church order is – the deployment of the whole church so that it may be engaged where it matters.

Words for setting apart, ordination, order, etc., are in the first instance words which apply to the whole church.[18] The community of faith has to be where it matters, at the right time to bring its impact to bear; and its forces need to be so disposed as to have maximum effect. Leadership exists to subserve this goal. The work of leadership is to enable the Christian community to serve effectively.

Two sets of questions may highlight a difference which underlines different concepts of leadership:

Here is one set. How is the enemy deployed? What dispositions do we require to contain his thrusts, anticipate his strategy and make a breakthrough? Where should the main troop concentrations be? Who will make a good commander for this or that part of the field in this particular engagement?[19]

Here is another set. Is the pattern of deployment in the best classical tradition? Who should give and who should receive orders? What eminences should be occupied by commanders?

Church leadership had no role except to facilitate the fighting of battles which God wants fought.

Then, coming down to earth, what alternative do we have to hierarchies or bureaucratistic equivalents? What alternative pattern is desirable?

There is no one alternative pattern. Patterns are developing all over the world. We are back in times like those of the early church. The volcanic fires of the gospel are changing out of recognition what were familiar ecclesiastical landscapes. The most obvious

thing is what is not being given attention – we must sit at the feet
of the world church and discover how God *is* disposing his forces.

Wherever there are areas of freedom, and the church is in movement, varieties of ministry are being worked out which provide
pointers. It is a time to discern what forms of ministry are meeting
the challenge of the new age so that the whole church can reshape
its life – always with the understanding that ministry is likely to
be different in different parts of the world just as it has been
different at different points of history. Even within one situation,
we must be prepared for differences.

A member of ZOTO, the people's organization in Tondo, the
shanty settlement in Manila, was asked about leadership in that
large community. He replied: 'We make sure that old leaders
are quickly discarded if they begin to feel too secure and sure of
themselves. We must always be encouraging new leadership to
emerge and giving these new people the opportunity to develop
skills. We believe that a whole community can take charge of its
own destiny – it does not need a small, specially trained and skilled
group on whom it must depend year after year. That way you only
get power blocs and prevent genuine leadership from emerging.'

Ministry is service within the people of God which ensures space
for the working of the Holy Spirit, so that the gifts he gives his
people might be recognized and nourished, and so that the many
ministries of the whole Christian community might be brought
into play. God chooses to extend his blessing, to restore and renew
his world, largely through human agents and agencies. Ministry
is a means whereby he deploys the resources of all his people so
that the world is blessed. Ministry is thus directed to concrete
change affecting the whole fabric of society and of personal life
– although in some restricted and constricting circumstances, the
scale on which this can happen will be limited.

Alternative forms of ministry are sprouting everywhere in the
world church. But there is scarcely any desire, in my experience, for
a new Protestantism, for an Alternative Church. The historical
failure of splits, like that of the Reformation, lies before our eyes,
and gives warnings which are being heeded. So there is still time
for the meeting, on an equal footing, of the traditional and emerging leadership to discern authentic ways of ministry for the world
church. This is now needed, and opportunities to bring it about
must be urgently seized.

## NOTES

1. A similar point may be made about prisons, hospitals and social services – while one may sympathize with officials in their difficult jobs. *The Guardian* of 5 March 1974 notes the case of one of Britain's most dangerous criminals, Walter Probyn. While serving a twelve-year sentence for shooting at police while on the run, he complained that the authorities suppressed his efforts to do anything positive while he was in custody. The docile prisoner, hospital patient and pensioner are more easily handled – and are to that extent more dehumanized than those who are in some sense awkward, creative characters.

2. However, material improvement may be needed to help people to begin to lift up their heads. Food which prevents brain damage, food and medicines which transform previously worm-infested bodies, can deliver from overwhelming listlessness and allow a new spark of life to take hold.

3. Hans Ruedi Weber, 'Freedom Fighter or Prince of Peace?', *Study Encounter* 32, vol. 8, no. 4, 1972.

4. T. S. Eliot, 'The Rock'.

5. A group which draws in upon itself, withdrawing from life and building up its spiritual stocks, may not be unworldly, but worldly in the worst sense. It may also withdraw in such a way that its withdrawal is an expression of concern – and so its spiritual life can be an expression of true worldliness.

6. Of course, this sense of solidarity in sin and restoration finds expression on many other continents too. In the tribal areas of Taiwan, before the Japanese occupation in 1895, adulterers, men and women, would lose their lives – the shedding of blood was needed to make good the damage done to relationships within the community. When, in this century, the practice gradually changed into one of levying fines, a man could be ruined – because everyone in the community, whatever its size, had to be compensated in order that solidarity might be restored.

7. It may be that, only when the social dimensions of sin are taken seriously, will the personal aspects be taken with fresh seriousness. The emphasis which has been placed on personal morality by religious bodies, with a very blind eye turned to commercial and international morality, had encouraged young people to see in sexual relationships an area of freedom in which they can move without restraint while concentrating on the major issues. Once these issues get the attention of the whole community, they may see more clearly the sin of mutual sexual exploitation and of reducing the depth of sexual meeting to superficiality.

8. Yet many of the things people perpetrate upon one another go, as hidden poison, into generation after generation before they erupt. How long, O Lord, how long?

9. e.g. the All Africa Conference of Churches; among others, Presidents Kaunda, Nyerere and Numeiry rejoiced to see this day.

10. Those who, when the terms of trade were in their favour, lauded the virtues of free world market forces, seem reluctant to take the point that

now, with the boot on the other foot, what we are beginning to see is the emergence of a more truly free world market.

11. Workers on the Continent, who are held up to their British counterparts as model participants in rational arrangements of industry, in fact look with both envy and hope to their British comrades. They have no equivalent to the shop steward. They are much more 'taken into the system'. The more ruthless forms of management and ever more meaningless work routines have more chance of establishing themselves, in return for swollen pay packets.

12. See Isaiah 1.5; 31.6; 59.13; Jeremiah 5.23; 6.28; Hosea 5.2; 9.15; II Kings 8.20, 22 and II Chron. 21.8, 10.

13. Heb. 9.10.

14. We must be on guard not to repeat what happened at the Reformation when those who knew that God was giving them a new way of life denied the possibilities of the new to others who did not fit in. The 'Magisterial Reformation' in George Hunston William's phrase (*The Radical Reformation*, Weidenfeld & Nicholson 1962) had no patience with untidy movements like the Anabaptist.

15. Thus, where direct political colonialism fails, economic colonialism may prove more effective. Tourism, which seems a godsend to stagnant and impoverished parts of the world which have natural beauty, can be Satan masquerading as an angel of light. Church authorities who know they can no longer hold a laity submissive may provide means for organizing and training them – which keeps one end of the rope in the same hands, even though it is a longer rope. What developing countries need in relation to tourism is space to take it in their way, in their time, to their benefit. What lay people need most of all is to be trusted to get on with the job of living out the faith in this world, discovering new community with one another and with the ordained as they undertake the task.

Of course, space and movement are nothing in themselves. Space could be space for chaos to come again. Movement could be movement to destruction. If a dominating power is overcome and expelled from life, this can make room, not for life-in-freedom, but for the return of the original oppressor with seven even more evil dominating powers. That saying of Jesus (Luke 11.24-26) also reminds us that oppression need not always come from external forces, it can also result from our own natures.

16. It can even get to this pass – a finance agency saying 'We have money in hand: can't you think up more ambitious schemes to find outlet for it?' This finance-determining-of-objectives is a particular temptation in countries which have a church tax levied by the state.

17. Churches in negotiation about union err gravely if they seek to find how they may combine the best gifts of ministry exercised in their separate traditions. Ministry can never be developed on the basis of a negotiated agreement – it is always an assignment of the Spirit based on the gifts of the Spirit, it is something churches discover as they move forward to bless men.

18. Note how Dr Hans Ruedi Weber has worked this out in relation to the meaning of baptism. See *Salty Christians*, The Seabury Press, New York, 1963.

19. We could learn a great deal from football strategists. It used to be the case that, if a star player was dropped for a match, he applied for a transfer. Now it is accepted that, for a particular match, the star player may have to give way to someone who is inferior over the whole piece because, for that particular match, a different style of play is needed. If bishops with star ratings could be dropped, hierarchies might be viable. But then, if such profound change took place, would they still be 'establishments of sacred rule'?

# III

## Hard Road Ahead: 'Be Salted with Fire'

The big question facing the West is whether the rich can be saved. By a process of repentance, renewal, amendment of life – spelt out in concrete attitudinal, economic, political and social terms – can the good news of God's delivering and restoring action bring the peoples of the world into a genuine and lasting community? That question is particularly directed to the northern part of the world from which so many of the influences which have dominated other people's lives have flowed.

It is a season in which the church is called to bear fruit before its time. Can we hope that the church will be a prophetic instrument to turn people to righteousness? If it is willing to respond to this calling, it will be in for turbulent times. The pressures within its own ranks, if it should face up to the challenge, will be very formidable. Ways of escape will be abounding and attractive. Only a church which is willing to lose its life will find it.

### 12 The Role of Rejection in Response

The youthful king of a country was preoccupied with his army, new technical inventions, everything that spoke of movement and power. The ruler of a distant kingdom, who had been a friend of his father's when he was alive, died, and the young man went to the funeral. There he met the king's daughter, brought out of the convent in which she was being schooled, now groomed for the reins of office. She was very young and very lively and vivacious, quick in mind and speech; and he was deeply attracted. A few months later he returned for her coronation. There was now no doubt about it. He was in love.

Shortly afterwards, she accepted an invitation to look around his kingdom. He showed her his stables, his chariots, armour, weapons of war, soldiers, scientific departments, industries, fleets. He took great pride in displaying these marvels, and laid them all at her feet by asking her to marry him.

'Why?', she asked. 'Because I love you', said the young king, 'and, besides, look at the strength our kingdoms would have if they were united!'

But she rejected him, and returned to her own land.

Over the next few years, other possible brides presented themselves. Many were more beautiful, some were richer than his first love. But just when he was on the point of offering marriage, something held him back – a memory, a vision.

As the years went by, good tidings flowed from the kingdom of the young queen. She loved people, and encouraged them to use their gifts so that humble homes were gay with the work of folk's own hands, and humble people had a voice. The ruthless elements of societies were checked. The destitute and the old were given place and honour.

The young king was worried in case she might rebuff him again, but at last he took his courage in both hands and wrote a letter asking if he might visit her and see her kingdom, of which he had heard so much good. He received a warm and welcoming invitation to do so.

She entranced him more than ever in her maturity. All he saw of her kingdom delighted him. He kept alert to the possibility that there might be an opportune moment once more to ask her hand in marriage. Then:

'Will you marry me?' she said.

'Why?' he said, before he knew the words were out, taken quite aback.

'Because we have been in love all this time, haven't you noticed?' she replied.

'But I thought you did not feel that way. You refused me. Why did you do so?'

'For love. When you asked me to be your wife, you were so wrapped up in your own kingdom and so proud of its accomplishments that mine would have been nothing to you. Love demanded separation until there could be real meeting. Now love seeks the partnership of our persons and our kingdoms.'

In 1972 the governments of the DDR and Poland agreed to allow unrestricted tourist travel between their countries. A group of young Poles and Germans met to look at this new opportunity for developing relationships, and gauge its significance both for their past history and their future. In a report which they prepared for their own reflection, not for publication, the following points are made:

German/Polish understanding is not a foregone conclusion, something that can be had without effort.... The previous history of German–Polish relations constitutes one immense failure to achieve understanding. The word that the Poles use to denote the Germans seems to sum up the history of such failures: they call him 'Niemiec', which means a 'deaf-mute' – with whom no communication is possible....

We cannot leave behind us the tragic history of the relations between our nation and neighbouring nations. Detachment from history is not only not permissible, it is impossible. In neighbouring countries we will come up against it in a very concrete way. We must know what happened, and what Auschwitz, Lidice, and Theresienstadt mean even at the present day. A start of new relationships and discussions is offered us despite past history.

A German reflection was offered as follows: 'We Germans must admit that it is not surprising the Poles have reservations about our sense of order, not only because they have a different mentality, more inclined to improvisation than to organization, but also because they object to foreign masters putting their house in order, and above all because in history they have learned to their cost the inhumanity to which thoroughness and order can lead.'[1]

Dealing with the past in the present for the sake of a more hopeful future is something which is incumbent on hemispheres, not only on nations. Philip Potter, General Secretary of the World Council of Churches, made the following statement recently:

... the relations between the north and the south over the past nearly 500 years has been one of economic exploitation, political dominance, racial discrimination and cultural imposition on the part of the north, thanks to superior technology and weaponry.[2]

The damage done to other peoples of the world by the northern races has not really penetrated the mind and spirit; and an enormous and crucial job of conscientization and self-education must be tackled in Europe and North America. But if this is done, it does not mean that a changed relationship can be easily established and accepted. Just as white liberals find themselves rebuffed by Africans in southern Africa – who believe they must take their destiny into their own hands, and that all that white liberalism may succeed in doing is blunt the cutting edge of their aspirations – so those who desire to establish worthier relationships on the scale of hemispheres, may be harshly rebuffed. An adjustment of step and an invitation to walk together will prove to be much too superficial a remedy to redress the complicated damage done in past history. There may well need to be an interval of rejection: a space for exploited people to recoil away from those who have dominated them, a space for the consciously or unconsciously arrogant to recoil from their past in shame. The mills of God grind slowly. Deep wrongs cannot be lightly redressed. 'Keep out until you have learned better' notices may have to be posted, the flow of money and personnel from one part of the world to another stopped. The need, in some cases, for a moratorium, a break in the flow of money, personnel, etc., from the richer parts of the world to the poorer parts, as has been noted, may not be a hostile action but an action for survival and identity. Where the mere presence of Europeans[3] makes for oppression, then their best service will be to get right out and to offer those they have sought to serve time and breathing space to develop their own particular way of Christian life. If the result turns out to be a time of helpless suffering, of breakdown, that may be the gift that those who have been only too dominating owe to the dominated.

That is what was experienced by the Sabaneto Community in the north of the Dominican Republic. They number about ten, and in an area where the struggle is to get up to subsistence level, they have to live from hand to mouth, with, at best, irregular employment. Yet they are Christians who have been made aware of their situation and have become convinced that they should not be victims but rather agents of change in it, in the hope that the whole area might become one of greater justice and opportunity. This awakening was stimulated and encouraged by the service of people from other lands. But the day came when they believed they had to part from their last expatriate worker and, with him, from the skills he brought and the finance which can always be tapped when someone comes from a richer land. Some time later they were asked:

'Would you like to have the help of expatriate staff again?'

They thought a bit. Outside help had obviously done a great deal for them. Then, one by one, they gave the same answer: 'No. It has been a painful experience, it has been a bit like death. We have often not known how to carry on. But we now begin to see, at last, that there cannot be resurrection without this death, and we are becoming resurrected as a community who make their own decisions, even though what we can do seems to be so inadequate in face of the needs of this whole area.'

The government of Panama announced its intention to fill all responsible posts which had been occupied by people from other countries with Panamanians. This was intended at first to cover church as well as state offices. It affected the members of the San Miguelito Community. The people feared a collapse of the enterprise. 'What will happen if you now have to leave the country, and we are left without you?' they asked the Chicago priests. Soon they said: 'But, hey, this just shows how dependent we are on you.' Then, 'What's more, you have been phasing yourselves out at the time you choose. That's not good enough! You are here to serve this community. We will decide whether and when you leave.' Finally they said, 'We are taking over.'

In Port Moresby, Papua New Guinea, expatriate missionaries and New Guineans meet in consultation. The missionaries want to hang back. They say nothing. The silence becomes heavy. So they initiate discussion. The New Guineans still sit silent. The thinking goes forward on one strong white leg and one weak black one. It is not that the missionaries want it that way. It simply has become the habit. Experience has shown that if there are two white people on a committee of twelve, they still dominate – whether they want to or not. They have so much fluency, they have techniques at their finger-tips, they are never short of ideas or plans or organizing abilities. 'How', said a missionary in despair, 'can we remedy the situation? Is the best service we can render to these people now, to go right out of their lives?'

Nothing less than an interval of rejection may be necessary to persuade European churches, which have comforted themselves for so long on the generosity of their programmes of service and aid towards others, to ask themselves drastic questions about the secret dynamic of their actions. Are they colonizers by the very fact that they bring with them advanced techniques, or welfare and health 'bribes'? Have they been unconsciously making assumptions of cultural superiority? Are they still downgrading certain gifts and life-styles which do not rank highly measured by their own norms? Are they, in the last resort, still acting as big daddy, with control over the purse-strings? Are they at all facing up to the first responsibility they hold, in their own part of the world – to persuade their fellows to disgorge the affluence once obtained by robbery, now continued by using as cheap labour the human resources of poorer lands? The northern world must look to countries which have long looked to it – for a rejection of its way of life powerful enough to enable it, so prodigal in its expenditure of the family inheritance, to come to itself and set its own house in order. Without rejection which really sinks home, how can we in our part of the world hope to repent of the evil, and express thorough-going amendment of life?

## 13   *The Role of Paralysis in Action*

Three brothers, very different in character from one another, were known for their wisdom, in a large area of villages. It was a dry territory, dependent on a few springs which were concentrated around one spot. So when the water became sour, unpalatable, and, when you were close to it, strange in its smell – though not poisonous in any way – the three brothers were approached for help.

The first brother gathered people around him and said: 'You realize that there is nothing wrong with the water as far as supporting life is concerned. What we must do is adapt our way of life, so that the taste and smell do not put us off. All we need is firm discipline. Then we can use gratefully what God has provided for our good.' So he taught them to adjust their standard of taste, and deal with the smell, holding their noses as they drank. Life continued. But the people longed for untainted, refreshing water.

The second brother, meantime, had busied himself. He had gone to the cities, to the men of science, to find an additive which would improve the quality of the water. He found what he wanted, but it was expensive. So we went around pleading the cause of the village people; and eventually collected enough money for a month's supply. The villagers hailed his return with relief and, in a few days, built a small dam to contain the water reserves so that they could be treated. Clean water flowed out. Everyone was happy. As the end of the month drew near, the brother went to the city again to ask for more money to buy a fresh supply of additive. But this time people said to him – 'We gave the villagers a chance. Now they ought to be able to pay for the supply themselves.' When he came back empty-handed, the people – who had suffered from bad crops and bad business – could not or would not provide the money that was needed. So the water went back to its old state.

Both brothers were angry at the third one, who was doing nothing. He had chosen a shady spot by the main road leading into the area. There he meditated and talked to passers-by. Week after week passed, and he did not so much as lend a hand to his two brothers in their efforts.

One day, when he came back home at sundown, they accosted him. 'Have you no compassion?', they asked. He gave no answer. 'Look,' they said again, 'we have tried this and that and bent all our energies to helping the people, and can see no way through. What have you done?' The third brother then replied quietly, 'The villagers will get good water.' 'No thanks to you, if they ever do', said the first of the two brothers. 'Would you like to know what I have been doing?', said the third.

'Once water has become unpalatable, there is little one can do to produce a permanent change, unless one gets to the source – which, for us, is out of reach. Surely, if you had taken time to think, that would have dawned upon you. The only hope for this area is finding fresh springs of water. I meditated long, and became sure of that. My next question was, "Why do people travel this road?". Some for business. Some for pleasure. But many because, whether they still live here or not, they once spent their life in this area, have relatives whom they visit, think of one of the villages as their home. I saluted everyone, and asked those who knew about this area where alternative sources of water might be found. Today I met an old man who told me of a group of wells which had once supplied hundreds of people which were covered over in a sand-storm. The water now used was easier of access, and they turned to it instead. Tomorrow we will dig where this man says. There will be fresh water for the people and for their children.'

It is instinctive on the part of Western man, when he finds one way blocked, to search energetically, even frantically, for an alternative way. It is death to stand still. The pressure of time passing, of wasted opportunities acts as a goad. Thus he has to live secretly burdened with unaccepted rejections, unabsorbed despairs, un-digested griefs. He cannot wait to chew the cud of experience and be nourished by it. So he moves hurriedly from a world too little penetrated by the basic realities towards some alternative world equally little penetrated.

An example is found in the missionary enterprise. For decades now there has been an awareness that something has gone wrong. The need to revise assumptions and attitudes has become pressing. Yet the time since that dawning has been marked by all kinds of attempts at adjustment which treat the old springs as the only reliable sources. The inadequacy of this is being pressed home by those who have been 'the receiving countries'. They point out that there may be no return of health, in specific instances, until every-thing seizes up and is brought to a halt.

In the Old Testament those on whom the awful reality of their people's conduct bursts like a thunderclap sit down *'astonied'* – that is, paralysed, speechless, horrified, dumbfounded. In the Hebrew, the ideas of surprise, fear and desolation interplay. Strik-ing instances of the dawning of horror will be found in Ezra 9.3 and Ezek. 3.15 and the prophecy of it in Jer. 2.9-13 and 4.9. The tearing of clothes is used as a gesture of revulsion from the past and rejection of it (see II Kings 22 and 23, which pivot on the verse 22.19). Job's three friends, on meeting him, 'wept aloud, rent their cloaks and tossed dust into the air over their heads'. Then 'for seven days and seven nights they sat beside him on the ground, and none of them said a word to him; for they saw that his suffering was very great' (Job 2.12, 13). In the drama it took that time of silent desolation to prepare them for the great debate which followed, on suffering and righteousness.

Men continually live accommodated to a reality which they have dressed up in familiar clothes so that they can cope with it. When an invading and strange reality inflicts itself upon them, there is a halt, a dislocation, a crisis. This tests people. Their reaction may be to tidy the new event into an old framework and explain it away. Or they may be prepared to deal with it openly and honestly – then they will have to face the consequences of confusion, disorientation, a future which becomes a question mark. This kind of situation occurs in the New Testament in relation to Jesus' authority. Was he not familiarly known as the carpenter's son? The tag, 'The Carpenter's Son', allowed him to be pigeonholed. Suddenly a larger reality shattered the manageable stereotype (Mark 1.22; 6.3; 7.28; 10.24; Matt. 7.28; 13.54). What were men to do? They were no longer safe. They were compelled to react for or against him. One can see the same dilemma in his own wrestling with man's unbelief and the Father's will (Mark 4.40; 6.6; 9.15; 14.32, 42).

The church is a human instrument and, through history, it domesticates God's new order, takes the sting out of his radical requirements, shuts up the kingdom. God in his grace is always willing to bring his church face to face with reality so that her ways may be amended. But this inevitably brings confusion, disorientation, uncertainty about the future. The ark of God will be in jeopardy. The church must secure it in some way, fast. Get a new image. Start a new style.

But may not confusion, disorientation, an unknown future be gifts of God? May it not be a blessing of God to be brought up sharp, prevented from making any progress, forced back on one's heels or on one's knees?

At certain points in the developing life of mankind and of the Christian community, something much more profound is needed than adjustment and experiment nakedness before God, helplessness. A psychological shock, a break from the past may be the appropriate treatment for an ancient burden of guilt and shame. A time of helplessness may be needed to free people eventually – not simply into *activity* but into *fruitful forms of reflection and action*. It was only after Elijah had digested the despair and grief of his defeat at the very moment of victory; only after a long journey and a crisis on a mountain, that he could get a fresh vision of God. Only when the grief and the vision were absorbed was it possible for him to hear his marching orders – to go back and change the political and religious situation, recognizing resources in it of which he had not been aware, or had neglected, or had despised (I Kings 19).

Alternative activity by itself may simply be an escape-mechanism, a form of cheap consolation, a screen to hide the disruptive and dehumanizing consequences of certain kinds of action from one's eyes. When the 'benefactor', the 'handout' man recognizes that he is a bankrupt, or even a criminal, there is the beginning of hope.

Hope cannot be dissociated from a time in the dock and a period kicking one's heels in jail.

## 14    *The Role of Non-communication in Prophecy*

A manager, recently-appointed, was undertaking a round of inspection in the Upper Clyde Shipyards. In common with all who work there, he wore a safety helmet. Its distinctive colour indicated his position in the firm. He came across two men sitting in silence, eating, and drinking tea.

'What do you think you are doing?' he asked.

They continued eating and drinking without a word.

'What right have you to carry on like that at this time of day?' he challenged.

They continued as before, without a word, without looking up.

The manager felt that he had to assert his authority in the situation. He was at least due respect and attention.

'Do you know who I am?' he asked sharply.

At last the silence was broken. The workmen looked at one another, not up at the manager.

'A man wearing a hat like that,' said one laconically, 'and he doesn't even know his own bloody name and what he's here for!'

Black theology is wine thrown in your face.

Latin American theology is a party where the guests speak to one another and ignore you, who presumed you were the host.

It is being driven home.

The good wine of the gospel is not ours to hand out.

It is no longer our party.

Those who have been disinherited by Western ways of thinking, by Western interests, academic norms, methods of organizing meetings and conferences, are challenging the assumptions which give their own characteristic ways of going about life a low rating. On what basis is the indirectness of approach of Northern Asian Chinese inferior to direct, logical argument where each point is developed in a straight line from the preceding one? Does not the characteristically African way of prowling round a subject, instead of going directly to it, gather more riches from its wide sweep than can any frontal assault? What about the Latin American way of meeting which leaves people to get into relationship with one another and, then only, quietly moves towards the work to be done – is the work not done, in the end, at greater depth because a basis of real personal relationship is considered to be important? On what ground should books have a higher rating than communal learning experiences and reflection on concrete struggles? On what basis can it be maintained that colonialist languages and the framework of reference that lies behind them provide instruments for world thinking which other languages lack?

But surely an effort in understanding can go some way to bridge these gaps! After all, there may be a real willingness on the part of those who had acted as if their ways were superior, to listen to alternatives and give place to them.

The crucial point is this. Whatever is available in comprehensible words is undisturbing to the foundations of thought. It leaves one with one's existing vocabulary and experience intact, and with the overmastering temptation to fit new things into these. What is now needed is a new hearing, new eyes, a new understanding. One cannot edge forward into radically different attitudes. Shock is needed; rupture.

Ears are closed to the cry of silence. Where individuals or peoples have been rubbed out, despoiled of their humanity so that there is no spirit, no resistance in them, there is an affront to the world as God has created it. Indians in America, blacks in South Africa, aboriginal nationals in Australia, West Indian children in Britain have been raising to humanity the cry of their silence, without having it heard. It is the calling of a prophetic minority to graft new eyes and ears on the unheeding majority so that they become aware how millions upon millions have been and are being robbed of life. The silence of peoples whose faces and bodies have been made blank should have set all the alarm bells ringing. But, at least from the time of Amos until now, it has not done so, even among those who acknowledge God as Lord and man as their brother in him. If the language of silence is not heard, and the urgent language of speech which points to it is ignored, the only way of hope may be shaking and shocking events. A sign of such events, and to some extent an event in itself which may help to bring people to their senses, could be a refusal of people to communicate, as long as the ground for communication is staked out by others.

Threatened, as they have been throughout history, with the humiliation of being merely fitted into the systems which have dominated for so long – if not of being rejected outright as primitive and barbarous – theologies from disinherited parts of the world are now asserting themselves. *They bring the terms for appreciating them with them.* These are not to be found in other histories and cultures. The desire of Europeans to communicate with them may accordingly register as simply one more threat of continuing domination. The plea may turn out to mean: 'find ideas, terms, concepts which will allow us to bridge this gap from where we are'. When this is so, efforts to communicate can be justly interpreted as an invitation to accept continuing dependence, as assertion of the finality of the old norms. To respond will do nothing for those whose theologies are being worked out in lives of sacrifice and suffering in the Third World. It will do nothing for Europeans and Americans, who need to get new perspectives and depth into their action and reflection that they may buckle to the job of changing attitudes and priorities in the Northern Hemisphere. Noncommunication will more truly register the reality of an exodus from the Egypt in which so many theologies have been imprisoned for so long, and help all parties to face it.

Consider. If what you hear is given in words, especially the words of your language, you will imagine you have opened yourself to the reality behind the words, when the very facility with which you have heard the words is blinding you to that strange reality. Wherever such a possibility exists, those who are concerned with genuinely indigenous theological thinking must perforce turn their backs on others for a time. They must concentrate on involvement and reflection related to their own history, and give one another challenge and support in this. Then what they do will clearly not be being made subject to judgment and validation from elsewhere. If they do feel the need to say something to others, to converse with others (for, after all, the shaping of theology is an action within a world fellowship) those with whom they dialogue must be prepared to shift from their own familiar and trusted ground. They must be prepared to understand, not just words, but a different history or different histories. They will need to be ready to take with deep seriousness world experiences which are very different from their own. They will need to move to a different kind of commitment in world history. They will have to be ready to have cultural scales ripped from their eyes.

The experts have once again been proved wrong. Stones which the builders rejected are becoming headstones. It takes a revolution in thinking and in relationships to accept the new order. For those who believe the old theologies were definitive it will be a self-crucifying process. Without death by crucifixion, world theology cannot emerge!

But non-communication is a very frail instrument for the dawning of new revelation. It does not disturb the power base. If only a substantial shift of power from the industrialized world to the developing world could be counted on, the pressure towards new relationships and manifold communication in a world society might be invincible. But the dominance of the wealth and technology of the old world does not look as if it can be cracked easily at this point of history. So there is all the more urgency that the Christian community should accept a prophetic role in the old world. It is here, in Europe and America, in the place of strength, that the most deep-going change is needed. Here must be the main place of mission, for the sake of the whole world. The calling is like that of Ezekiel 'whether they listen or refuse to listen, say, "These are the words of the Lord God"' (Ezek. 3.11). There must be prophetic words and actions in the hope that people might hear and change and be saved. But it may take events, a shift of power, catastrophe, before peoples will take seriously what is required to bring the world into line with God's purpose.

The calling and its consequences are deep-rooted in the nature of Bible prophecy. Among the most difficult passages in Old Testament and New Testament are those related to the calling to speak words of prophetic importance *in order that people may not hear and understand and be converted*. Recourse is often made to theological trepanning to ease the impossible pressure of conjecturing that God, in making his ways known to men, could harbour such a horrifying and illogical intention. A surplus attribute has had to be invented – his permissive will. God wills things to happen which are illogical or contradictory – but only in the sense that he is prepared to let things happen instead of stepping in to prevent them. The Trinity is a permissive society.

It lifts the strain.

But the biblical words are more intransigent. They leave no doubt that this form of prophecy is to be made so that it acknowledges or even produces ears which do not hear and hearts which do not understand. That is, one is called to prophecy which is an exercise in futility; and one remains committed to it when the futility is apparent. This was the character of the mandate given to Moses in his confrontation with Pharaoh (Ex. 4.21; 10.1, 27). It was an integral part of the prophetic role which Isaiah was called to fulfil after his great vision (Isa. 6.9-13). It provided the terms for Jeremiah's calling and mission (Jer. 5.20-22). Jesus Christ does not come into the world to sit in judgment on the world (John 3.17); but he is come *for* judgment, to give sight to the sightless and *to make blind those who see* (John 9.39). He himself comes not to judge the world but to save it; but his word carries its judgment with it (John 12.46-49). The word which was his life-declaration robbed people of sight and hearing (note the secret of the parables indicated in Mark 4.10-12), as well as bringing new life to others. The prophecy of Isaiah is fulfilled. The presence of Jesus *binds* and looses men (Matt. 13.14-17).

Paul wrestles with the difficulty (e.g. Rom. 11.7, 8; 9.14-18). He tries to make sense, in terms of God's sovereign power, of prophecy which seems to have such an arbitrary impact on people's seeing and hearing. But his argument trails off into ineffectiveness.

It may be that, in our time, the history of non-European peoples illumines scriptures which have been substantially closed to us. From new sources there comes the word of prophecy; and a *necessary part of it is to produce incomprehension*. What happens when words have so lost their power and credibility that they have no capacity to produce repentance and amendment of life? They must not be set aside, they must still be spoken: because one day they may be able to bear their full weight again. One must even cling to the hope that their weight may come through with sufficient impact to make people hear and see. Then prophecy will be no longer simply word but itself word-event. However, it may take more radically disturbing events to make sufficient impact. A profound shaking may have to take place in the history of the world to change deep-rooted attitudes. The prophecy by word and by sign (e.g. Isaiah's walking naked and barefoot, Isa. 20.1-6) must be given its time and opportunity to make impact. But, for how long? It may be 'until cities fall in ruins and are deserted, houses are left without people, and the land goes to ruin and lies waste, until the Lord has sent all mankind far away, and the whole country is one vast desolation' (Isa. 6.11, 12). Disaster and exile may have to intervene. *Only then* may the words of prophecy come alive and find soil in which they can get nurture and make growth.

What we are being told in these difficult passages is how prophecy works. What we are being warned about is what it will mean if we are to be prophetic today. We might have hoped that prophecy would be a clearer and simpler activity.

But it is not.

What blunted the edge of prophecy time and time again in the past? Assimilation to the existing system (a confrontation between radical and conformist prophecy is set out in I Kings 22.10-28). The unhearing ear, the hardened heart reject the genuine prophet, bring him up sharp time and time again, force him to reckon cruelly with what is in men. So authentic prophecy develops more and more realism, both about the nature of man and about the power of God, the more it encounters rejection. Prophecy gains stature and clarity from the rough time it is given. That is a gift from 'unhearing'.

If authentic word and sign are not enough, what is then left? It is sometimes observed that Marxism is pretty ruthless about the individual life as long as historical standard-bearers of the hope of humanity press victoriously into the future. But God's way with man appears to be just as ruthless. He takes a long view. It may take generations for a word of prophecy to strike hime. The effect of prophecy may be only to make people more self-enclosed – until some event comes which shatters their complacency, and with it the world which they had constructed as a bastion of security for themselves. Evidently humanity under God has to undergo long experiences of rejecting the reality for which he stands until something happens which allows new light to penetrate, new priorities to be accepted, and new ways of life to be essayed. Prophecy has to be such that it either produces positive response, or that it effects that kind of hardening of heart *which hastens the only alternative hope* of the opening up of human beings to reality – a shaking of the foundations. What matters most is that, one way or the other ('whether they will hear or whether they will forbear') human beings do face up to reality.

## 15   *The Role of Conflict in Shalom*

The visitors gazed admiringly at the machine.

'How beautifully proportioned it is, a real work of art', they said. 'It is not doing its job', said the craftsman.

'How smoothly it works', said the visitors. 'It is not doing its job', said the craftsman.

'You must preserve this', said the visitors. 'If it should get destroyed, you may never get anything like it again.' 'It is not doing its job', said the craftsman.

So the craftsman went to his drawing board and laboured until he had designed a machine adequate for his purpose. He broke the machine the visitors had admired, put the pieces into the furnace to melt them down, and added fresh metals to give new resilience and strength. Then he poured the metal into moulds and carefully trimmed and polished each part so that it would fit in smoothly with all the other parts and do its distinctive job in the total operation. Then he assembled it. He tested it out. It seemed to be working effectively. So he coupled it up.

At first the machine shuddered as it took the strain. The parts had not yet settled into one another. He wondered if it was going to shake itself to bits or blow up. Then it buckled to the task. The wild vibration eased. The speed and power increased. At last, it was operating at maximum, fulfilling the task for which it had been made.

The craftsman sighed a sigh of relief and gratitude. 'She is at peace', he said.

\*    \*    \*

The word 'shalom' may be a difficult word in English, but it has qualities which are important. It suggests a unity which comes from different parts not just fitting in with one another, but shaped and set together so that their very differences, strains and tensions interplay to produce power which allows a work of purpose to be done. The word retains a strength which 'unity' and 'peace' may have lost.

The challenge to ecumenical advance today is being quite mis-read. It is so often represented as a search by the churches for common ground on which they may stand and common fields in which they may co-operate. It is, rather, to be so engaged in bringing the world towards the purpose for which God created it that all the risks are taken of the church's being torn apart. Christians will take different sides when they get into the battles to change the present world order into the order of God's promise. They will split down the middle about how to handle different issues. The big ecumenical question is not whether they can develop more harmonious relationships. It is whether they have enough in Jesus Christ to hold them together against all the odds. Similarly, in direct relationships with one another, they must respect one another so deeply and sincerely that they can take one another by the throat about the things that matter.[4] It is a mistake to believe that Christians should be polite to one another. What they do owe to one another is courtesy. Courtesy has been an honourable word in the English language, at least as far back as Chaucer. It means having deep respect for other people – so deep that you are prepared to tell them openly and honestly what they need to know for their good instead of glossing that over to smooth things out. The way between Christians should be that of honest and open speech which is humble and yet unvarnished. So Jesus spoke. So St Paul took the young church to task. So the young church took him and fellow members to task. What mattered was the kingdom. There needed to be straight relationships between those who were committed to it.

The options are these:

You have an unrenewed church which is split apart and cannot function as the bearer of healing.

You have a church in which different denominations are drawn together on the understanding that the most controversial issues will not be raised. Unity becomes a security-device to preserve church life. A church at peace within itself in a world of disorder is a testimony against the gospel.

... 'not as the world gives ...' John 14.27.

Peace, you deceiver,
giving
all you profess:
changing
red-blooded human kin of God
– mind, spirit, fire –
to drowsing trees
or chirping on their stems
while suns swing by

> peace, you seducer
> luring
> from true spouse Christ
> saying
> 'Teresa yes. Camillo, no!'
> – one part undone –
> 'Piety, yes,
> home, job – a world that plain
> people can grasp'

>> peace, you betrayer,
>> sucking
>> heat from the fight
>> twisting
>> to devil's own exegesis
>> 'love', 'promise', 'grace' –
>> dealing in guile,
>> the knave card 'Reconcile!'
>> at Truth's straight flush:

peace, you bright bastard, leave us
that peace of Christ receive us.

You have a church which is radically engaged in the struggles of men for a new world. A church torn with disagreement because it is committed where it matters, prepared to be broken for the healing of the nation is a sign of hope and of ecumenical maturity. Is not the sacrament which nourishes the church in its ongoing life a sign that it is through brokenness that humanity might reach out to wholeness?

So the big ecumenical question is this: is the Christian community prepared to take its place in the transforming work of God, each company within it fighting for the truth as it sees it, opening its convictions to the judgment of others, and staying in the family?

The reaction in many parts of Europe to the Programme to Combat Racism remains instructive. Look now at what happened from a particular angle. The churches, through the World Council of Churches, could make resolutions for twenty years, each building up towards a point of commitment. No one was worried. There were no headlines. But once the churches, through their agency, put their money where their mouth was, all hell broke loose. That the programme was designed to help and strengthen (more by moral backing than anything else, because the finance involved was not really significant) despised and downtrodden people all over the world was scarcely noticed. Only where the affluence and security of whites was threatened, was there an outcry.

Those to whom it never occured to ask about the extent to which money given by their government to support countries abroad actually found its way into instruments of control and suppression,[5] suddenly became alarmed that funds given for educational, medical and social purposes by the WCC might be diverted and used for armaments. Veterans of two world wars suddenly became pacifists – not on behalf of themselves but on behalf of distant Africans.

There have also been honourable, thought-out reactions to the Programme. There are wrong ways for the Christian faith to find expression in political commitment – the Northern Ireland case must continually be before British people. But the alarming thing is the extent to which Christians have a belly-reaction which they identify as being against 'the churches' involvement in politics' and is merely the expression of a conservative political stance. It is alarming how little Christians in one part of the world seem even to think they need to listen to Christians in other parts of the world where the balloon has gone up. It is alarming that a threat to personal interests and attitudes is so often interpreted as a threat to the pure quality of the gospel.

The church is no longer an insignificant force in the secular world, as it was in the first century AD. It is involved politically, whether it wants to be or not. Cardinal Heenan, who in a letter to *The Times* before the last British election, resorted to the old 'goodie/baddie' categories for Christians and left-wing 'extremists', as they were being called, was not acting as a neutral adviser but as a supporter of a particular party – as some of his denomination soon pointed out. Other church leaders, who about the same time urged reconciliation in industry, tried to pour holy oil on troubled waters without asking whether they ought to be troubled, indeed more troubled, until a fairer form of society was established.

What is God doing in this world? Is he not subverting the present order of things to establish the order of his promise? Is he not shouting people in to work with him in the work? To discern where mighty things are at stake and to be agents of change in the world so that it is transformed, is surely the normal calling of the Christian. It is not our calling to leave things as they are. We have no right to let the good biblical word 'reconciliation' – which suggests a surgeon cutting deep into where the trouble is before he cleanses and heals the wound – be watered down until it means 'not causing trouble because we're Christians'. Politics is simply one of the activities people need to undertake to organize life, when it is on a greater scale than is possible in face-to-face relationships. The question is not whether the church should be involved in politics, but only how. The more unthought-out its positions are, the more it reacts to preserve its interests and then finds moral or theological justification for doing so, the more it is simply a worldly church, drifting or self-enclosed, a stumbling-block to the kingdom.

But to get thoroughly into the issues which are concerned with the establishment of dignity and justice for humanity as a sign of the deliverance God has promised, will be to face controversy and turbulence. Christians will not only take directly opposed political positions, but they will find it difficult, on the basis of the same faith, to stay in community with those who take up contrary positions. That is probably one reason why the church shies away from the crunch-point so often, and substitutes strongly-worded resolutions for sacrificial living.

As the church must be committed in the struggle for righteousness in the world, so it must be committed to a struggle for the truth with fellow Christians of many different persuasions. Unless we take one another to task about the dark forces in our denominations which produce complacency and self-regard, and which make others write off the church as no sign of the life of Jesus Christ in the world; unless we probe behind the positions of 'less acceptable' churches to discover real things they stand for behind the more dismissible appearances – we have no hope of shalom. At this point of history, the fight should really be serious between evangelicals and catholics, conservatives and radicals, pacifists and guerillas – it is neither good enough to be split for the truth, nor to pull punches to keep unity. One of the signs of the church as the first fruits of a new world is the way in which all these different expressions in the life of the church are beginning to open towards one another and their advocates work together in certain limited fields. This may spread. Understanding-in-the-truth could grow. It is getting quite rare in a situation in which some change towards righteousness is being brought about, to find Protestants and Roman Catholics in different camps, or Christians separated from non-

Christians who hold similar perceptions about the need for a work of transformation. Ché Guevara said that the Latin American revolution would be irresistible when Christians joined in in such a way that they neither used their situation to impose their dogmas on others by proselytizing, nor hid their faith by just fitting in tamely.[6] Something similar must happen to the different parties in the church – there must be engagement in the mission of God to bring the world to his purpose, and this must mean Christians working together so that they neither use their common task as an opportunity for proselytizing in favour of their own position, nor play down their beliefs as if there was nothing to fight out.

Finally, behind all this, there must be a struggle with God. God has to be taken to task by man. He has a dark side to his nature which contradicts so much else. He is callous, revengeful, despotic, arbitrary, domineering. He treats men in a way which makes them poor, lording it over them, always taking the initiative and deciding what the question should be: while man is left in a position in which he can say little more than 'Yes, sir, Yes, sir.'

In Romans 9, Paul argues that this is right and proper. Man is properly at the mercy of God's over-ruling will and should submit to it. He is simply clay in the hands of the divine potter. Commenting on verses 19 following, Professor James Denny says: 'But human nature is not so easily silenced. This interpretation of all human life, with all its diversities of character and experience, through the will of God alone, as if that will explained everything, is not adequate to the fact. A man is not a thing, and if the whole explanation of his destiny is to be sought in the bare will of God, he *will* say "Why didst thou make me thus?" and not even the authority of a Paul will silence him.

'Man is not clay, and the relation of God to man is not that of the potter to dead matter ... or the moral significance is taken out of life.'[7]

Job is the Prometheus of the Bible, standing up to God, demanding an explanation of the dark things and a recognition of himself as a person with place and dignity.[8] Abraham had to haggle with God against the indiscriminate ruin which would attend the destruction of Sodom and Gomorrah, skilfully arguing God out of his vengefulness (Gen. 18.17-33; even if the fate of the cities was sealed in the end, that Abraham was prepared to stand up to God in the name of justice and mercy shows what being the 'friend of God' should mean). Jacob bargained with God (Gen. 28.20-22) and was not frightened to stand up to him and wrestle for his life and destiny (Gen. 32.24-30). Moses disputed with God over his calling to release the children of Israel from slavery in Egypt – successfully developing an argument, stage by stage, to show that he was the wrong man for the job, (Ex. 5.3, 4; in the dispute he had a clear points victory over God – in spite of which he failed to get the referee's verdict!). Jesus contended with the Father about the wastefulness of the sacrifice his life implied, on the road to Jerusalem (Mark 10.32-34), and then in Gethsemane, where his sweat was like great drops of blood because of the severity of the struggle (Mark 14.32-42).

Why is there a need to stand up to God and challenge the fairness and rightness of his will?

Does God not need, from fellow workers with him in his work, people who have an independence of mind and a capacity for initiative which characterizes their whole life – not only when they are face to face with fellow-men but when they are face to face with him? Do they not need to mature in their understanding of his ways by opposing them?

The fruit of our struggle with God may well be to discover the coincidence between his purposes and the fulfilment of our own personal beings and of our societies. Thus Abraham, bargaining with God, as he thought, to reduce the terms which a tyrant would impose upon those who merited his anger, may have been in fact on a voyage of discovery to find the nature of God's judgment and mercy. The fruit of Jacob's wrestling was a new and enhanced identity and place in God's purpose. Once Moses took the road to deliver his people he found that he was equipped as he went and was able effectively to do what he had effectively argued was impossible. Jesus disputed the will of the Father, holding himself open to the possibility that that will held the true meaning of his life: so as he was led to take a sure, sacrificial road to salvation for humanity. The kingdom is to be taken by storm. Those who fight God to the last ditch may wrest from him what he has in store for them as a gift. Only if we are prepared to unmask God and find his name is it possible to discover our own.

## 16   The Role of Powerlessness in Change

'Brother go my way, my way's the right way,
brother go my way – your way is loss.
Brother go my way: if you don't go my way,
brother for your own good, I'll hang you on a cross.'
    So spoke tyrants all down history,
    statesmen, clergy imposing their will:
    bosses, parents – but when we're rid of them
    drifting, guideless, we long for them still.

'Brother go my way, my way's the right way,
understood rightly, your way is mine:
I'll go your way to get you where I want
you'll find your freedom, falling in line.'
　　So spoke wise men all down history,
　　knowing better than others their good:
　　but, without them – starved of confidence
　　we'd sell freedom for some of their food.

'Brother go my way, my way's the right way,
Brother go my way – your way is loss.
Brother go my way: if you don't go my way,
brother for your own good, I'll hang on a cross.'
　　So spoke Jesus back in history,
　　spent for others, for love was his crime:
　　his way tempts us: but doubts keep entering –
　　will that way work, and pay off in time?

Brother of the byway, your way, my way,
must gain a highway else we are lost.
Can there be one way, we can take humbly,
that way a through-way for God paid the cost?

Everyone has a gift for changing the world. Some have the gift of
power. Some have the gift of powerlessness. Those who see in Jesus
Christ the ultimate power and have seen that expressed in his self-
emptying and servanthood, know that it is not their place in society
but their relationship to him which gives them means of handling
life effectively, so that it is a blessing, not a curse, to mankind.
　　Sympathetic Marxists say of Christians that they are much too
unrealistic about power – much too undisciplined about getting
down to the job of discovering where true power lies, how to
secure it, and how to use it to achieve desired ends. For the
Marxist, power is the one necessary tool for effecting change. If
you want change, you work out how you can get your hands on
power. A proper criticism of churches and Christian bodies is
given at this point. There is so often a failure to get down to the
hard business of analysing situations, finding where change is
needed and how it might be effected, discovering what levers must
be pulled – and, producing a realistic plan so that you get hands
on these levers. One of the best examples of the effective use of
pressure to produce change was when a Central African Federation
(which might have made Zambia and Malawi into Rhodesias as
well) was contemplated. Dr George MacLeod roused the Iona Community, who roused the churches, who roused the nation – and put
sufficient pressure on the government, from this side to meet up

with the pressure coming from Africans – so that their voice was heard. The hard work of discovering the facts, checking them, presenting them, was efficiently done. The case succeeded, against all the pressures applied by government to discredit it. But it is only too rarely that the churches do a thorough job of homework on situations, discovering the power-points and pressure to effect change towards justice.

Those who do not have access to power have the gift of their powerlessness as a provision for effecting change. Powerlessness has been mainly identified with helplessness before situations – in spite of the fact that Jesus Christ, as a powerless man, changed the world. Peoples of the world are awakening to the fact that they need not accept life as it is. There appears to be some strange confidence which basic people have gained today, – a vision of what life might be like and an awareness that means for its realization starts at their door – a conviction that the universe is on their side. The opposition may have the most overwhelming military hardware. But if it does not have the universe on its side, it is the weaker party.

Let us be realistic. Powerlessness in itself effects nothing. Powerlessness without hope all over the world finds expression in attitudes of despair, in listlessness, in opting out. But add hope to powerlessness and the situation is quite changed. Existing orders soon learn to recognize the threat. Powerlessness allied to hope represents an invincible force.

What is the importance of this force?

(*a*) Those who hold physical power can exercise strict control over the lives of others to gain ends they have set themselves. But how are these ends related to the purpose for which the world exists? If human life is made in the image of God, and if the world is the bearer of his purpose for mankind, there will be a lasting quality about the ends that those in power prescribe *only if they are subservient to that overarching purpose*. On the other hand, those who are committed to that purpose and are convinced that it is the prevailing one, although they may have no physical power at all to back their convictions, have something more durable: they know what life is for. It is those who have a sure touch for reality who have the one unbeatable thing in the flux of history.

(*b*) To change life through powerlessness, has more hope of eliminating hate and of preventing alternative oppressions once the tables are turned. The relentless build-up of truth-force (Gandhi's Satyagraha) may leave the pretentions of military force exposed, in disarray and confusion. The build-up of such an approach cannot be haphazard or merely instinctive. It takes organization, charisma and good timing; resolution to cope with disappointments, ill-luck, intimidation, shows of force and threats of force. A small guerilla band in the hills may seem to be in a hopeless position in face of the resources of a colonial power: but if it expresses the aspirations of the people who are lifting up their heads and seeing the prospect of a worthier life, the physically weak sign may be for the over-throwing of kingdoms.

In the history of the Quakers or Friends the compelling thing is not that they rejected war. This itself was only an interpretation of something deeper. They stood for implementing the truth as they could discern it, without compromise, when and where they were. They were stoned, sawn asunder, afflicted, tortured. But what they put into history has been more effective and convincing than a multitude of armies.

Something like that is happening in our day, with the additional element that there is developing a world-awareness. Those who are convinced that quite drastic changes have to take place in the present order are supported and challenged in a great world-company. All over the earth people are struggling to regain control over their lives, or to establish it for the first time. They are aware that things need not be as they are. They had consented to their own enslavement, and are now determined to throw off that yoke. What is happening is not a planned and concerted movement controlled by some central agency. Rather one senses deep tides of human assertion. People believe that their destiny should be in their own hands, and will no longer allow it to be in other hands.

Power needs powerlessness, and powerlessness needs power. They are not alternatives. When Gandhi advised the Congress Party to dissolve when Indian independence was won, he did not see that just as power needs powerlessness to help correct it and bring it to the bar of justice, so powerlessness needs power to provide institu-tional means for a changed and changing way of life. Powerlessness is open to the weakness of making concessions too early – which undermines the quality of victories; and of giving up or handing over to less scrupulous hands the machinery for managing a better order once it is ready to be brought into being.

What does the longing 'would that all God's people were prophets' mean today? Might it not mean that, just as Nathan, Isaiah, Jeremiah, Peter and John stood up to authority in the name of the Lord in their day, so a sign of the kingdom exists where people in the name of the Lord confront power-structures in our time? This was deeply at the heart of the marches that the San Miguelito Community made upon the government in Panama. It was a central motivation in the risings in Madagascar in 1972 and 1973 which brought out people of all kinds into the streets of Tananarive – young and old, labourer and middle-class – and produced such solidarity that the poorest people pushed students behind them shouting 'You are our hope for the future' and bared their own breasts to the guns. It is the resource of the Tondo people in Manila, who have no weapon but their powerlessness and their vision of a different life to bring to bear. Many laymen and pastors in Korea are being imprisoned because they stand for a different society; and the very imprisonment has its effect to shape the future. Australian nationals ('aboriginals') contrasting the low status that they have in their own society with the dignity ascribed to them in the gospel, are on the march to bring a truer society into being. Leaders of independence movements in Papua New Guinea had to break away from the church in order to find space in which to operate and interpret their political role; but they acknowledge the source of their vision, inspiration and driving force in the gospel. All over Latin America, the belief that God the Lord has promised better things is causing people to lift up their heads, shake off the yoke and through a quiet build-up of strength under oppressive regimes or through guerilla bands in the hills, venture their lives for a new world.

Christians are to do the truth, not attempt to reduce truth to spoken words. Wherever the truth is done, something exists that is stronger than armies.

The Holy Spirit is the source of truth. He will not let unreality gain and hold the field. He keeps bringing it face to face with reality. Wherever reality confronts unreality, even if all the advantages would seem to be on the side of the latter, a force for change is let loose. The agents of the Holy Spirit have no right to be anything but catalysts and disturbers, who help the powerful to see their weakness and the powerless to understand their strength.

## 17 The Role of Conscientization and Dialogue in Mission and Evangelism

In his own way, he was happy. He had been blind and deaf since birth. He had a corner in which to sleep, food which, some days, was sufficient for his needs, and kind people who were prepared to give time to while away the hours with him.

He asked them about the world and how it was getting on. Through a language of touch which they had developed, they built up the picture. There were many fine things in the world but, for good reasons, they were not equally distributed. There were superior types of human beings who had a right of access to a larger share, and inferior types of human beings who naturally got less. It might seem to be all wrong that God should make two different breeds of mankind. But it came right at the end of the day, because, at death, God balanced things up in a life beyond.

The trouble started when the Healer arrived. He examined the man's eyes and said 'Would you like to see?' Through hand language the message was transmitted, and an excited and affirmative answer given. The Healer put ointment on the eyes which had been blind and after two days the sight began gradually to return. The Healer went on his way. A few weeks later he found himself in the area once more; and met one of the villagers who had acted as translator. 'How is it with my friend?' he asked. 'Bad', came the reply. 'Why?', asked the Healer with concern, 'has he lost his sight once more?'. 'He has recovered his sight completely, more's the pity!' 'Why do you say that?' 'He is no longer the happy man he was. He has looked on those who live in misery around him and has looked on those who live in abundance. He says there is no essential difference between them, that they are of one humanity; and that life is unjust. It hurts him. He is not at all the contented man he was.'

The Healer continued on his journey, and found that it was as he had been told. He sat down with the man again. Through an interpreter he asked 'Do you want to have your hearing restored?' The villagers intervened. 'You have done enough damage already', they said, 'leave the man in peace. We will look after him. We will see that all that he needs is supplied. Only don't cause him more distress by giving him back his faculties.'

'Do you want your hearing restored?' asked the Healer of the man. Less excitedly but still with conviction the man asked for restoration. In spite of the opposition of the villagers, hands were laid on him and healing ointment applied. After two days, the hearing began to come back and the Healer left.

It was a month or two before the Healer returned to the village. When he was seen, a group ran towards him in unconcealed hostility. 'Was it not enough', they asked 'to rob a man of his peace, that you had to rob him of his faith as well?' 'What do you mean?', asked the Healer. 'Now that your patient can hear, he has learned of other religions, other understandings of God, other explanations of life's meaning. He no longer has something sure and definite to hold on to that can act as an anchor for his life. He has become restless, he distrusts the understanding of life which his forebears and we ourselves have handed on to him, he searches in every religion and every form of belief to find a sure basis. He is a disturbance to us all.'

Just then the man saw him in the distance, ran to him and embraced him. The Healer turned to the group. Looking at the man he said 'They tell me that I have robbed you of happiness and security by restoring your sight and hearing.' 'They have told you some part of the truth', said the man. 'I am no longer happy as I was. I am no longer secure as I was. Only now I am alive.'

To many today there seem to be two particularly serious threats to the work of evangelization. There is conscientization, which offers the threat of identifying the gospel with revolutionary activity to overthrow existing orders. There is open dialogue with people of every kind of faith and ideology, which suggests losing the cutting edge of proclamation.

What is evangelism? The announcement of good news. But who announces this good news and brings it home to human beings? Jesus Christ himself. This would be widely agreed. Yet, in practice, the announcement of himself made by Jesus Christ is closely tied up with the announcement men make of him. If Jesus Christ is the one to choose the place and way and time for making himself known, then to be an evangelist is to be ready to be told to keep out of situations, to wait on the sidelines until required, to be where you are wanted but with your mouth shut, to say what has to be said whatever the consequences. It is a big strain to be alert and available for whatever might be one's part in Jesus Christ's announcement of himself. Evangelists are only too easily tempted to cut the knot and choose their own time and manner and place of announcement. Evangelism must also mean that people can come alive to God in ways which do not conform to those which the evangelist prefers – the temptation is only too obvious that the evangelist will want converts to adopt his own life-style. What is called evangelism turns out very often to be proselytism, which came under Jesus' condemnation.

The word 'conscientization' comes from the Portuguese. In that language it combines two related words which we use separately in English. It stands for the development of a fresh awareness on the part of people who had previously been prepared passively to accept situations – the development of 'a consciousness', through an examination of the situation, that things are as they are because it has suited certain people to arrange them thus. But it does not stop at that. This 'consciousness' is allied to the development of a 'conscience'. Whatever is wrong in the situation is seen to be wrong in God's sight, and calls for change. The word came into currency through the work of Paulo Freire in Brazil. He worked out with the peasants a method of literacy, related to people's own use of familiar words, which broke down words into syllables which could be joined together to make many different ones. They could become literate in a surprisingly short time. But it was not for that that he was put in prison and then expelled from the country when the Brazilian military junta took over. It was because people were encouraged to use words and imagery which helped them to understand the character of their own situation and then to see what alternatives might be open to them. Such people become dangerous agents of change.

In the Bible, the world is declared to be God's. Men are, accordingly, not to be the victims of other powers, but servants of his. When they see the world as it is and are awakened to it as it might be, they become aware of the huge gap. They come alive and kick. Well, what is this contrast between a reality which demeans and dehumanizes and a worthier way of living which beckons – other than the pressure of the kingdom of God on our human societies? What is new life for men which gives them dignity and hope and a place of worth if it is not the first taste of that abundant life which Christ promised? To be delivered from fatalism into lively participation in transforming the world – can that come from some impact other than that of Christ the Evangelist?

A missionary in Panama, Ken Mahler, reflecting on the work being done in the Miraflores area said:

... the proclamation of the gospel is directly related to conscientization in this – that as people become convinced that they are children of God, redeemed at such a great price, they then acquire a dignity that should make it impossible for them to continue living in such a submissive and exploited fashion.

All along the line we have tried to present the gospel of Jesus Christ in a natural setting as the power of God that is at work liberating people, making life more human, bringing hope – and therefore a basis for action.

Serious dialogue with those who have very different beliefs from themselves is a fairly new step on the part of the churches. The churches have often, in the past, undertaken debate in order to discredit opponents of the faith, or to convert them. Dialogue sets itself neither aim. If you, as a Christian, enter into dialogue with a Marxist, or a Hindu or a Moslem, you do not choose the most favourable ground to press home your points; nor do you try to make your arguments prevail; nor do you manipulate the discussion the way you want; nor do you consider the whole time wasted unless you persuade the dialogue partners into your own camp. You enter into dialogue with the serious intention of understanding the position of your opposite numbers and bringing as sympathetic a mind to bear upon that as possible; of giving full weight to their position even if it is not too effectively stated; of exposing yourself to conviction by it; and of showing where you stand yourself. Dialogue is an act of courtesy, not an act of manipulation. What seems to worry some people is that it seems to suggest that truth can be found everywhere and in everything that anyone believes; and so the good news is being watered down losing its character and flavour.

Dialogue may mean carelessness about the truth – if it is reduced to giving everyone a chance to say his or her say and be listened to politely. But dialogue, in a Christian sense, is opening oneself to other people *so that the whole relationship being established is open to Truth*. In proselytism, the one taking the initiative is quite clear who is converter and who is convertee. In dialogue, undertaken as an act of faith, there is the hope that everyone concerned will be converted to the truth. In such dialogue the Christian may show his need of conversion through a Moslem or atheistic colleague – much more than that colleague needs conversion through what he has to offer. But essentially the intention of dialogue is that all parties should be converted to the truth. Instead of blunting the cutting edge of evangelism, this sharpens it. For it provides conditions in which human beings are saved from converting others to their own poor understanding of the faith and their limited appreciation of Jesus Christ. Instead they open up the whole situation before Jesus Christ so that he can make his impact. A serious and respectful listening to and talking between people who know that crucial issues are at stake in their conversation, allows Jesus Christ to be the evangelist to believer and unbeliever together. The human evangelist is then someone who points to Jesus Christ, not someone who possesses Jesus Christ and puts him on offer to others – there evangelism would slip into idolatry. For the Christian also needs conversion continually. After Peter had been well converted, and lived his life alongside Jesus, Jesus asked him 'when he had been converted' to strengthen his brothers.

The conversion to God of the believer at the hands of the unbeliever is of special importance. The continual process of conversion will certainly involve fellow-believers as well. But the language and manner of conversion experienced at their hands will not be so shaking and startling. The unbeliever is the messenger (angel) of God's unexpectedness. In the story of Cornelius in the Book of Acts, an apostle was converted by an enquirer in a drastic and dramatic way that affected the whole future character of the Christian church.

Conscientization and dialogue are necessary characteristics of the announcement of the evangel. 'Adapt yourselves no longer to the pattern of this present world, but let your minds be remade and your whole nature thus transformed. Then you will be able to discern the will of God and to know what is good, acceptable and perfect' (Rom. 12.2). If the right response to the hearing of the good news is self-offering, then one must refuse to conform. Evangelism rouses people to change the world.

Dialogue protects evangelism from becoming idolatrous or slipping into proselytism. Engaged dialogue is neither neutral nor indifferent in the search for truth; neither is it manipulative, bent on winning someone for a cause. Rather it offers free space for Jesus Christ to draw men to himself. The conditions for genuine dialogue allow those who take part to be neither uncaring nor dominating – attitudes which equally interfere with Jesus Christ's presentation of himself to men.

How does this work out practically?

No longer may the Christian see the work of evangelization as something belonging only to people with a particular calling or endowed with a particular gift of fluency. The announcement of good news has to do with Christians being found in all kinds of company, open to the understanding of life that may come from any kind of person – not using the company or the conversation to get their own oar in in a particular way, but to invite God to do what he chooses with everyone concerned. It means bringing people alive to a new order of things which expresses the coming of the kingdom and the doing of the will of God, on earth as in heaven.

## NOTES

1. A report translated from German by Halina Bortnowska.

2. In relation to the Bangkok conference 'Salvation Today' Dec. 1972–Jan. 1973.

3. Europeans bring with them expertise, fluency, health which may, without one word being spoken or one wrong attitude being adopted, make the people of the land feel disadvantaged from the start.

4. With regard to the Vatican's Concordat with the Portuguese government, a priest who was deeply involved suggested (this was before the coup) that it would be a great ecumenical advance if the WCC were to break off diplomatic relations with the Vatican until the Concordat was abrogated.

5. The latest instance before going to press is of the secret US stockpile of $5,000m. worth of arms in South Korea, South Vietnam and Thailand, recorded innocently as 'support of other nations', which ex-Senator J. W. Fulbright described as 'typical of the way the executive branch tries to get around congressional cuts' in arms aid.

6. ¿Fidel y los Cristianos, aliados?, Pastoral Popular no. 127, Chile, p. 3.

7. The Expositors' Greek Testament, ed. Sir William Robertson Nicholl, Hodder & Stoughton 1897, p. 663.

8. See especially Job 7.1-10 on the hard lot God has willed on man; 12.10-16 on God's brute power and 13.3, 4, 15, 19; 15.12, 13 on man's right to stand up to God and put his case.

# Summons

A call to take a significant part in the terrifying and healing mission of God is going out to the churches of the West, where main blockages to that mission are being discerned. The call is not coming from some Episcopal Conference or Ecumenical Council, nor is it set out in a coherent message. It is the cry of humankind concerned to survive and find significance in this world: and within that, the cry of the world church as it lives out its faith in suffering and fierce joy.

How is the Christian community in the West to respond?

Response must come from the roots of the life of the people. Yet at the roots there is so much apathy or paralysis. The temptation is strong to apply some spiritual whip. But movement generated from the outside has no permanece. What can stir and change the hearts of Christians?

1. They must be helped to live afresh in a world fellowship so that they grow new eyes and ears. Something must happen to eyes such as happened with African art; to ears, such as happened through the Beatles. African art, judged by familiar Western norms, was regarded, till the last few decades, as crude and primitive. But once it was received on its own terms, it silenced dismissive critics. The Beatles persuaded our ears to accept new ranges of hearing and to get accustomed to instruments which had once seemed exotic or odd. Our seeing and hearing as Christians need to be stretched and transformed. Books like Frantz Fanon's *The Wretched of the Earth*[1], projects like 'The Future of the Missionary Enterprise', Third World films and poems, stories and analyses given through direct voice on cassettes – these must become ingredients in our regular diet. Access is needed to the broad range of experience and outlook of the Christian community – to guerillas who have taken to the hills or to the urban underground, to those who feel they must work within tightly controlled regimes without confrontation. We need to hear and see Christians in situations of tension and opportunity living out lives which vividly interpret faith – especially where they are in solidarity with the broader human community and are a sign and promise to it. Only within a

hearing of the world church's life can the churches of Europe hope for a renewal of their own. The rawness of encounter must be retained. The temptation is always to sieve out the most upsetting elements. Then what is left becomes as innocuous and flavourless as baby food; and the ordinary church membership is once more patronized, instead of summoned.

It could take ten years or more for the difficult process of grafting new eyes and ears on to the old and begin to produce results. Lent – when we are so often left to gnaw the fingernails of our guilt without quite knowing why – could be chosen quite consciously as a time to walk with Christ and our brothers, bearing the cross of today's world.

No one can anticipate what will come out of this. The risks of exposure to realities must be taken. If what results is a more committed and conscious parochialism, then we must live with that. It is better to be hot or cold. At least the possibility is also offered of prophetic perceptions which may, in time, persuade us as countries and as churches to alter profoundly our relationships to the rest of the world. If this is not done in time, the other side of prophecy remains – the positive interpretation of shocks and catastrophes for the privileged as bringing within them possibilities of a more just and healthy community as bringing within them possibilities of a more just and healthy community for humankind. 'Whether they will hear or whether they will forbear' the calling to the churches of the West invites them to be agents of miracle. New eyes, new ears are needed to perceive and respond to what is happening in God's world.

2. In particular, the church is called to exercise discernment, one of the gifts of the Spirit, about shifts of power at this point of history which may make it easier to establish true community. In Britain there is a shift of power to industrial workers. This can be given an alarmist interpretation; or it can be recognized that, when we left political feudalism behind us, we retained many elements of industrial feudalism. This is being rectified by power more broadly based on the people and 'participation in government' by the basic producers of wealth. Abroad, God willing, there may be a shift of power to primary producers. If this lowers our standards in the West the church has the double opportunity of helping people to welcome a redistribution of the world's wealth which lets previously exploited countries benefit, and of taking much more seriously the plight of the poor in our own land so that what we have is fairly shared.

The establishment of true community in this world is related not only to shifts of power but shifts of people. It is a great new gift that so many of our societies can welcome immigrant communities. The world is being enriched.

3. There is homework to be done, once new priorities begin to be worked out. The announcement of the good news, which is the announcement of deliverance to captives and the opening of prison houses, is done not only by word but by factfinding, by knowledge of the processes by which decisions are made (from the local council to UNO), by discernment about where pressure can be effectively brought to bear, by good timing, by the constant scrutiny of forms of power and a constant search for valid forms. In this work, the whole church must become engaged. It must handle the Bible in fresh ways in relation to these challenges.

4. Missionary societies, structures for home mission, Christian educational establishments must be put on the rack. Why have grown people been for so long fed on mission milk instead of the red meat of mission? Why is mission at home and abroad so marginal to the life of the membership and so remote from the concerns of ordinary people? Why have our educational processes turned people out with consciences oriented towards the past rather than to the future, with parochial rather than world consciences? We need deepgoing change of mentality and of instrumentality.

5. There are resources in the middle class (which covers most of British church membership) as yet untapped. Their growing awareness of how people live in the world forces on them the contrast between the deprivation so many suffer and their own material wellbeing. Asked for charity, many are ready for sacrifice. This may be true particularly of the young, but not only of the young. In parts of northern Latin America you may hear, 'Paulo Freire is taken to be the patron saint of peasants. He is rather the saviour of the middle class. So many have found meaning and vocation in life by a radical identification with the poor'. Who would read this book? It is not in the language of workers. It expresses in its language, some kind of confidence in middle class response. Among the middle class there may be a special resource in clergy whose consciences have not been appeased through social activism, who are ready for a ministry which may mean risk, controversy, the setting before people of 'life and good, and death and evil'.

6. What organization should be developed to care for all this? None, I think. We have enough already: One for Renewal, the Iona Community, basic groups and communes inside and outside the church, many such. If the points set out herewith suggest to

some people essential objectives which they must pursue with more definiteness and dedication – let them develop initiatives from where they are and find resources around them, and get on with it. We have had enough of co-ordinating organizations which soon put on institutional weight and secure their own place and future – that death-in-life. What may be needed is sources for the nourishment of vision: Third World Centres, *New Internationalist*, the William Temple Foundation, Iona, Selly Oak, eager now to be of service not only to the Christian enterprise overseas, but the enterprise at home. Find and use them.

Why, in the end, look to the church, which has let God and man down so often?

Because of the life of Jesus Christ at the heart of it. It draws from him a capacity for repentance and amendment of life, and a capacity for self-criticism. The one who is at the heart of it keeps recalling it to its true vocation.

It must become what it is.

## NOTE

1. Frantz Fanon, *The Wretched of the Earth*, Penguin 1966.